My Most Memorable Teacher

My Most Memorable Teacher

100 Alberta Stories for 100 Years

Faculty of Education
University of Calgary

Commemorating Alberta's 100th birthday and
the centenary of teacher education in the province

Published by
Red Deer Press
A Fitzhenry & Whiteside Company
1512, 1800–4th Street S.W.
Calgary Alberta Canada T2N 1N4
www.reddeerpress.com

Credits
Cover and text design by Red Deer Press
Cover illustration by Leslie Bell
Printed and bound in Canada by Rapido Livres Books for Red Deer Press

Acknowledgments
Financial support provided by the Canada Council, the Government of Canada through the Book Publishing Industry Development Program (BPIDP), the Alberta Foundation for the Arts, a beneficiary of the Lottery Fund of the Government of Alberta, and the University of Calgary.

THE CANADA COUNCIL | LE CONSEIL DES ARTS
FOR THE ARTS | DU CANADA
SINCE 1957 | DEPUIS 1957

National Library of Canada Cataloguing in Publication
 My most memorable teacher : 100 Alberta stories for 100 years / Faculty of Education, University of Calgary.
"The Centennial Story Project."
Includes index.
 ISBN: 978-1-55005-177-3

1. Teachers—Alberta—Anecdotes. 2. Education—Alberta—History.
I. University of Calgary. Faculty of Education.
LA2321.M95 2005   71.1'0092'27123   C2005-905137-X

Contents

One of the most imaginative projects I have been involved with in some time is *My Most Memorable Teacher*, the Centennial Story Project of the Faculty of Education of the University of Calgary.

As you will observe from this anthology, the distinguished judges have made selections of the most worthy of the many stories submitted by individual Albertans from across the province recollecting their personal experiences with teachers who inspired them. It is a remarkable and valuable collection of Alberta stories.

My congratulations to all those who have contributed to this fascinating project: The Centennial Planning Committee of the Faculty of Education of the University of Calgary and their supporting team; the judges who selected the stories contained in this volume; the financial and promotional assistance from the Department of Education of the Provincial Government; and many others who have been involved.

Enjoy this remarkable collection written by Albertans in their salute to Alberta's teachers over the years.

Hon. Peter Lougheed
Honorary Chair
The Centennial Story Project

All of us had at least one special teacher who remains in our memory as a person who played a special role in guiding and inspiring us in the classroom and in our lives. Sometimes this memory comes from a dramatic episode, but more often it comes from the little things that happened day-to-day, or from a spontaneous moment. Quite often teachers may not even be aware of the impact they had, nor of the influence of the examples they set.

My Most Memorable Teacher, the Centennial Story Project has provided Albertans with the opportunity to recognize all of our teachers, over the past ten decades, who have given so much to individual Albertans and to our province. The 100 stories in this book recount some of the many contributions made by teachers working in facilities from one-room rural school houses to large urban schools. These stories are also about teachers who have faced a wide variety of challenges in a school day, yet remained dedicated to providing their students with the best possible education and personal support.

In 2005, Alberta's Centennial year, we reflect on the history of our province and the incredible contribution of our teachers, past and present. As such, and on behalf of Alberta Education, I am very pleased to support this project as part of our Centennial program and as a contribution to the University of Calgary's celebration of 100 years of excellence in teaching.

Congratulations and best wishes for another 100 years of educational excellence in Alberta!

Gene Zwozdesky
Minister of Education
Deputy Government House Leader

There are many ways to learn about good teachers and about what makes them so. One of my favourite ways is to listen to the stories that people inevitably tell about their experiences in schools and about the teachers they remember. I am intrigued that the public discourse about teachers often seems critical, yet so many of us remember teachers who make a tremendous difference in ours lives.

The memorable teachers you will meet through the stories in this book have inspired, encouraged, and redirected their students. They understood their students and believed in them and they went beyond their daily task of helping students master the curriculum. The students remember vividly the events they described in their stories. They draw courage and confidence from these memories years later, but the teachers do not always remember these specific stories. For teachers, these events are part of the way they relate to students every day, but unfortunately teachers are seldom told about the difference they make.

We hope that through this collection of stories we will encourage many of you not only to think about a teacher that was memorable for you but that you will also find a way to thank that teacher. Enjoy these stories and tell your own stories about memorable teachers,

Annette LaGrange, PhD
Dean, Faculty of Education,
University of Calgary

My Most Memorable Teacher
100 Alberta Stories for 100 Years

Celebrating 100 Years

The year 2005 marks two important Alberta centennials: a century of provincehood and a century of teacher education. On September 1, 1905, Alberta officially entered the Canadian Confederation as the country's ninth province. Less than three months later, on November 20, 1905, the government announced that the provincial Normal School would be located in Calgary. (The term "normal school" for early teacher-training colleges across North America signified a commitment to a high standard or "norm" of teaching that graduates would take with them to their far-flung schools.) This marked the infant Alberta government's first commitment to publicly-financed post-secondary education.

Over the past century, the Calgary Normal School evolved into the Calgary Branch of the University of Alberta, and later, as the Faculty of Education, became the founding faculty of the University of Calgary.

How do you celebrate a centennial?

You pay due attention to the intellectual and professional development of teacher education in Calgary and in Alberta over the past 100 years. You mark program changes from rudimentary four-month sessions of the early 20th century to today's full-service Bachelor of Education and post-graduate programs. You observe quantitative and qualitative increases in practice teaching or "practicum" experiences of teacher candidates. You acknowledge the importance of a century of partnership between faculty members and classroom teachers in preparing successive generations of beginning teachers.

You take the celebration out of its university confines and include the larger educational and civic communities of the city and the province. You plan a variety of activities designed to involve the community, encourage recognition of teacher importance, and leave a legacy for the future.

These activities included: a commemorative historical book, *Becoming a Teacher in 20th Century Calgary*; an interactive web site enabling alumni to explore links with colleagues from their graduating years; a University of Calgary convocation which celebrated the 100th graduating class of Alberta teachers, and awarded an honorary degree to Dr. Myer Horowitz, former Dean of Education and president emeritus of the University of Alberta, in recognition of his contributions to early-childhood and other levels of education in this province; and a Centennial Scholarship Fund to help attract the very best teacher candidates to the Faculty of Education through the 21st century, and serve as a legacy for the future.

And, *My Most Memorable Teacher*, the Centennial Story Project.

Who Was Your Most Memorable Teacher?

We invited all Albertans, past and present, to submit stories about their most memorable teacher. We asked: Which Alberta teacher from kindergarten through Grade 12 had the greatest impact on your life?

Every former student retains vivid impressions of memorable teachers. Some were inspirational, some funny, others tough but fair. Sometimes their impact lay in what they taught, while in other cases it was more intangible: how they taught and the kind of relationships they formed with pupils. We received dozens of inspirational stories of primary-grade teachers who were generous with their hugs when youngsters badly needed comforting, taught nose-blowing drills after repeated failed lessons at home, and guided frustrated children through that all-important breakthrough in reading.

Perhaps that most memorable teacher was your Grade 4 home-room teacher who created such a safe and caring environment that you could report the arrival of your new baby sister without fear of being ridiculed by giggling classmates; or your Grade 6 teacher from the "tough-love" school, who named you honorary president of the dreaded Beaver Club to encourage you to stop chewing the stub ends of pencils; or your elementary school principal who was a whiz at arithmetic, with a trick up his sleeve to help kids remember various math functions and applications.

Through junior high and senior high school, as generalist teachers gave way to subject specialists, we continue to cherish memories of those mentors who made a difference. Those memories may centre on physical education teachers who saved spots for us on the basketball team, guidance counsellors who helped us weather the trials and tribulations of teenage life, or science teachers who excited our imaginations and steered us toward university and future careers.

Do you remember your Grade 9 music teacher whose thorough teaching of Tchaikovsky's *1812 Overture* opened your eyes to Napoleon Bonaparte and Russian culture, as well as to classical music. That chemistry teacher famous throughout the school for reciting the periodic table of the elements backwards, and well known around town for constructing an atomic-bomb shelter in his basement. Or that Grade 12 English teacher, a stern disciplinarian totally lacking any sense of humour, who introduced you to the magic of Shakespeare's plays in literature class and the valuable skill of précis writing in English composition classes.

Hundreds of Albertans sent us stories about memorable teachers. These teachers spanned the various decades of the twentieth century, were well distributed geographically around the province, and covered all the grades from kindergarten to high-school graduation, all the subjects from language arts and social studies through Math 31 and cosmetology.

All stories for *My Most Memorable Teacher* were submitted to a panel of judges for adjudication. These judges, drawn from teaching, writing, and history backgrounds, carefully read the letters with the following questions in mind: Is the letter well-organized, clear and concise? Does it provide enough context to appreciate the particular teacher's impact: historical era, geographic location, school name, grade level or subject taught? Does the writer write passionately about the teacher nominated? Has the teacher had a profound impact on the writer over time? Is this a truly memorable teacher?

Choosing 100 letters for this anthology was not an easy task. Although dozens of excellent letters had to be dropped because of space limitations, they are available on our centennial web site, *celebrateteachers.com*. In the meantime, we invite you to sample those published here. You will be amazed at the "miracle workers" portrayed in these pages.

Thanks and Appreciation

Special thanks to Hon. Peter Lougheed, former Alberta premier (1971–1985), who served as Honorary Chair of the *My Most Memorable Teacher* project. Mr. Lougheed proved unwilling to sit back and bask in the glow of "honorary" chairman; instead, he was a most active participant in the process. He delivered an inspirational message on the importance of teachers at our September 2004 launch ceremonies. And he was the first to contribute his own memorable teacher story—an account of how his high school physics teacher helped shape his future political career.

Thanks to judges Marianne Fedori, Jessica Grant, Richard Heyman, John Howse, David Jones, Ethel King-Shaw, Anita Li, John Sayre Martin, Peter Menzies, Katie Pallos-Hayden, Virginia Stephen, and Amy von Heyking who proved so diligent in reading and appraising the submissions. The Centennial Story Project steering committee members Noel Jantze, Calgary Public School Local, Alberta Teachers' Association; Alexandra Jurisic, Calgary Separate School Local, Alberta Teachers' Association; Pat Gillespie, retired Calgary Board of Education administrator, and Jean Hutchison, Alberta Retired Teachers' Association, provided valuable advice and guidance to the project.

Sincere thanks to the Alberta government and its representatives for graciously supporting this and other centennial initiatives of our Faculty. The Community Initiates Fund provided general support for our 100th anniversary activities. Alberta Education provided funding for distributing copies of this anthology to schools and libraries across the province. Special thanks to Dr. Lyle Oberg, Minister of Learning, and after November 25, 2004, Gene Zwozdesky, Minister of Education, as well as to Don Tannas, former member of the legislative assembly for Highwood constituency.

This project received strong media support. Daily and weekly newspapers, radio and television stations throughout Alberta helped publicize this project. We particularly appreciated Tony Tighe, who became our media champion in helping us promote the project. And finally, special thanks to ACCESS: The Education Station for its public-service spots and to the *Calgary Herald* for running weekly Memorable Teacher stories throughout 2004 and 2005.

Senior University of Calgary officials provided support for this and various additional centennial projects: Chancellor William Warren (whose father, Dr. Robert Warren, was a 1925 graduate of the Calgary Normal School and "memorable teacher" for many Alberta pupils); President Harvey Winegarten; Roman Cooney, Vice-President, External Relations. Special thanks to Dr. Annette LaGrange, Dean of the Faculty of Education, for her consistent support of Centennial projects. Graduate student Jean MacEachern provided invaluable "detective" work in tracking down missing information.

Finally, this anthology would not exist without our authors. They answered our invitation for submissions, sent along photographs and other illustrative material, then waited patiently while our panel of judges sifted through hundreds of delightful stories from the past. This anthology presents their heartfelt, personal stories of inspiring teachers, rather than the usual authorized approach to educational history. Readers may encounter descriptions of teaching and learning more appropriate to past decades than to the present day. In the end, however, we have 100 grateful authors who salute 100 memorable Alberta teachers.

Three names appear at the end of this introduction. Jennifer Diakiw, Communications and Development Director, Faculty of Education, conceived the idea of the *My Most Memorable Teacher* project and supervised the many facets of the activity. Project coordinator Maureen Washington provided the necessary communication skills to ensure publicity for the project, organizational skills to keep the paper flowing, and editing skills that guided the finished manuscript through production. Robert M. Stamp chaired the Centennial Planning Committee of the Faculty of Education.

Jennifer Diakiw
Maureen Washington
Robert M. Stamp

Faculty of Education
University of Calgary
June 2005

Chapter 1
Pioneer Teachers, 1905–1930

The new province of Alberta faced a pressing demand for qualified teachers. In the sixteen-month period from the onset of provincehood in September 1905 to the end of the calendar year 1906, Alberta organized 184 new school districts and witnessed an 18 percent increase in pupil enrolment. The province moved quickly and decisively to produce well-prepared teachers for this burgeoning market. In November 1905, less than three months after the inauguration of the new province, the Alberta government announced that its teacher-education college or "normal school" would be located

Calgary Normal School, 1908–22. Covering an entire city block between 4 and 5 Avenues and 6 and 7 Streets Southwest, this building later housed McDougall Elementary School and is now Government House South. *Courtesy: Glenbow Archives, NA-2293-1*

in Calgary, and would accept its first students in January 1906.

Young people, seeking admission to normal school in Alberta's early days, needed but a high school diploma and a guarantee of moral character from a clergyman or other "respectable" person. After a brief four-month training session of theory classes and "practice" teaching, most were hired by small, rural school boards to teach all the children in all the grades in one-room country schools. Many of these (mostly female) rookie teachers were but 17 or 18 years old, away from home for the first time, equally frightened and brave, ready to spread literacy and enlightenment to the far-flung regions of the province.

With additional normal schools established at Camrose (1912) and Edmonton (1920), teacher supply gradually met demand, and Alberta grew less reliant on teachers trained elsewhere to fill its classrooms. During the 1920s, admission requirements were strengthened, and the training course was length-ened from four to eight months. Still, young and immature graduates of the normal schools faced formidable challenges in their first years of teaching—crowded classrooms, isolated schools, few opportunities to share experiences with friends and colleagues.

This chapter presents four memorable teachers from Alberta's pioneer years: Lora Wickson, Bradley Stocks, Jean Ross and Elizabeth Smith. Despite over-whelming numbers and challenging situations, they fostered learning, helped youngsters overcome obstacles, and encouraged pupils to make the most of their lives. Wickson, Stocks, Ross and Smith are models from an earlier time who continue to inspire.

A Little Girl Who Needed Love

by Martha (Conner) Wedgwood

Lora Wickson
Ehnes School, near Nemiskam

It was a bleak time in our household in 1924. Mother had died a week before my eighth birthday. My eldest sister became the home-maker for the family. My other sister had to stay home that day to help with the washing and ironing.

I walked to school—alone.

Miss Wickson, my teacher, often walked down the hill with us when it was home time. I liked her and always tried to please her. This day we walked alone. She held my hand. "Are you sad? I saw you wipe tears away today."

"I miss my mother," I cried as I brushed away the tears with the back of my hand.

"Let us sit on this rock and you can tell me all about it." With her arm around me, I sobbed my heart out. She wiped away my tears with her handkerchief. "Seeing it is your birthday, I have a little gift for you. You may open it now." She handed me a little box neatly wrapped in red paper. I opened it and couldn't believe my eyes. It was a gold-coloured locket with my initial on it.

"It is for me?" I asked.

"Yes. I hope you like it. Wear it today on your birthday."

Martha has kept her treasures for over 80 years. Lora Wickson (far left) with her brother and sister; and the locket. *Courtesy: Ron Bunton*

My arms went around her neck and I kissed her. I could not believe my eyes. I asked her to put it around my neck.

"There now, there it is—pretty."

I hopped and skipped all the way home, so anxious to show off my beautiful present to my family. There were tears in Dad's eyes as he put in pictures of mother and me.

I grew up and became a teacher, but I never will forget the teacher who spent her hard-earned money on a little girl who needed love and caring at a sad time in her life.

Beautifully Trained in England

by Thelma (Hare) Levy

Bradley Stocks
Josephburg School #296, east of Fort Saskatchewan

I remember Mr. Bradley Stocks as the best teacher I ever had. He came from England to teach at the Josephburg School in 1910 or 1911. I was still in the primary grades, using a slate for my lessons.

Mr. Stocks must have been beautifully trained as a teacher in England and he brought that English system to us. Each morning he opened school with a scripture lesson and a prayer. He also had the Union Jack flag raised and lowered, morning and evening. When the school day was done, we all stood by our desks and sang *Now the Day is Over*.

Mr. Stocks was strict—he had to be with a school room of fifty students and as many as sixty in the winter. He also had to teach Grades 1 through 8.

Mr. Stocks had musical training as well as academic. Our school had a

Thelma (Hare) Levy, circa 1918.
Courtesy: Barb Ferguson

portable organ which he played very well and, to my delight, he taught us musical drama. One Christmas it was a whole evening performance of *Red Riding Hood* and another year was *Cinderella*. I was "Cinderella" and Eddie Thomas was the "Prince". We danced the gavotte together. Can you imagine what a thrill these performances were to us children? Right then and there was born in me the desire to become a teacher and teach these musical dramas.

Mr. Stocks' teaching of math ("sums" he called them) was as thorough as his literature, history and composition lessons. He made Dickens' *Christmas Carol* and *Pickwick Papers* live for us.

He did a number of wonderful things for the school. He built up a library with good books—from fairy tales to the classics. My brother, Frank, read every book in that library and I came in a close second. Mr. Stocks had water-colours and pans imported from England. We were taught the primary colours and how to make secondary ones. Our Christmas cards decorated with holly and berries were cards of beauty for our parents.

I do not know where Mr. Stocks went or what became of him after he left our school. I do know that what I did with my life was taught to me during those formative years.

Smiles Beget Smiles

by Chic Miller

Jean Ross
Craig Murray School, near Cereal

The name Jean Ross is one I will always remember. She was a great teacher, not only in the classroom, but also for the example she set about life and living.

We lived in a very dry district, and the money for a teacher's salary was not always available, even though it was only about $600.00 per year. For this reason our country school did not open in the fall of 1922, so my older brother and I went to school in the town of Cereal. In January 1923 our home school of Craig Murray, with Miss Jean Ross as the teacher, opened, so Ted and I went back home.

In those days country schoolteachers would teach all subjects and Grades 1 to 8. Because the number of students was small, Miss Ross made an exception and agreed to teach my brother and me in Grade 10.

The Department of Education had full control of all exams higher than Grade 8. The only part played by the teacher was to hold the sealed papers and make sure that nobody saw the contents prior to the hour the examinations were to begin. This date was set by the department, and was the same across the province. A given amount of time was allowed, and then the teacher was to pick up the papers, seal them immediately and send them to Edmonton for marking. When the results were printed, some time later in the Calgary papers, my brother's name and mine were both there, but not one of our original classmates in the town school had made it.

This in no way indicated that Ted and I were smarter than the others. All the credit must go to our wonderful teacher, Miss Jean Ross. In fact, at midterm, when we left Cereal to go to the country school, we were on even terms with the rest of our classmates. All gain we had made was after we had changed schools and teachers. Miss Ross achieved this while teaching all grades while the town teacher had only Grades 9 and 10.

I think there would be no child who did not gain considerable knowledge by association with Jean Ross. I am not only referring to the A-B-Cs and 1-2-3s. Everything she did or said prepared us for life itself, outside the classroom.

The children had an open invitation to come back in the school room anytime during the noon hour or recess. We could discuss any problem or subject—not necessarily our schoolwork. I was one of the children who took advantage of this opportunity. The lessons I learned have been used more than the algebra she taught me.

One of Miss Ross' theories was, "The more you use something, the stronger it gets. There is no gain in learning something if you are going to forget it. So train your memory. Use it and the rewards may not be obvious at the time, but will be very helpful all during your life."

She didn't stop by just saying the words—we were always shown how to apply them. We were taught and shown it was not possible to plant weed seeds and expect flowers to grow. We were shown by actual experiments: if you are kind and thoughtful to others it will be returned, if not by the same person, then by others.

Sorry to have to say, I have never seen my special teacher since I was 25 years old, but have always tried to use her teachings in my life. I know she pointed me in the right direction, and it has brought good results—both socially and financially.

Try it sometime. When you are walking down the street, and meet somebody, look directly at them with an open smile. They will smile back. If not, they have never met Jean Ross. Smiles beget smiles.

Mrs. Smith's Legacy
by Martha (Nelson) Gathercole

Elizabeth Smith
Berryfield School, Sedalia (near Oyen)

As far as I was concerned, she was always old. I don't remember her hair being anything but snowy white, and she wore it pulled back neatly in a bun. Her name was Mrs. Elizabeth Smith and she was not only my most memorable teacher, she was the *only* teacher I ever had.

I like to think that her hair was white when I started school, otherwise it would be easy to believe that I was the cause of the transformation as I was a non-stop chatterbox. Mrs. Smith was a slight, regal, English lady who was aboard a ship on the way to Canada when the First World War was declared in 1914. She would not have had any idea what lay ahead for a young schoolteacher who was coming to a new land to marry her childhood sweetheart.

From 1924 to 1937, Mrs. Smith taught Grades 1 to 9 in the one-room Berryfield School in east central Alberta; teaching up to fifteen students at a time

Elizabeth Smith. *Courtesy: Tom W. Smith*

including her own three children. I started school in 1927 and, as all the desks were filled, I had to take my own little green chair from home until a proper desk became available.

Mrs. Smith had unlimited patience as she impressed upon our young minds how important proper diction, grammar, spelling, penmanship and books were. She had a knack of making stories come to life when she read to us. We could almost see the explorers reaching shore and enduring hardships as they crossed our beloved land. Mrs. Smith was also a great lover of poetry; one of her favourite poems was *What is So Rare as a Day in June* by James Russell Lowell. Poetry has been a very enjoyable part of my life, thanks to my teacher.

Each year Mrs. Smith organized us to perform a musical play, and involved the whole community to prepare the stage, props, and costumes. We naturally did British plays like *Dick Whittington*, but I especially remember the Cinderella story. The older boys, as footmen, sheepishly wore their mothers' brightly-dyed bloomers along with their rubber gumboots (they did not own shoes), crepe-paper jackets, and white pleated ruffle collars stiffened by dipping them in milk. These costumes were the source of much hilarity for the students and audience alike.

Martha's nature book. *Courtesy: Martha Gathercole*

The most valued memories that I have of my school years, though, are the year-end picnics when Mrs. Smith took us to Jimmy Ford's coulee. We would take our lunch and walk nearly a mile across the prairie where we would all sit in the shade of the trees and enjoy the treats that our teacher had bought for us. The coulee was an oasis on the vast grassland. Saskatoon bushes attracted many species of birds and flowers not ordinarily seen. In fact, that is where I saw my first Cardinal with its bright red plumage and black throat. The student who saw the most birds and could identify them in Mrs. Smith's bird book would get a special treat, and this created plenty of fun and interest for all.

This love of nature has stayed with me all of my life. I still have in my memento box—a "nature book" that I made in 1931. It is filled with pressed flowers and weeds of the prairie and all are very well preserved after seventy-four years. For my effort, I received a leather bound autograph album with a verse written and signed by Mrs. Smith. The album joins the nature book as two of my most prized possessions.

After all these years when I think back on my school days, it is not the frigid three-mile winter rides on horseback across the prairie to Berryfield School that stand out in my mind, but the pleasant times, the stories, poems, plays, summer picnics, and especially the love of nature that Mrs. Smith taught me that has provided me with so much pleasure all of my life.

Chapter 2
Teachers of the 1930s

Despite the economic collapse and human misery produced by the Great Depression, the 1930s proved to be one of the most innovative decades in Alberta's educational history. Desperate for funding and open to suggestions for radical social change, provincial educators proposed and instituted significant changes in a number of areas. To foster inquiry-based learning, school curriculum was turned upside down with the introduction of the "enterprise." To address the

Calgary Normal School, 1922–40; today called Heritage Hall, part of the Southern Alberta Institute of Technology.
Courtesy: Glenbow Archives, NC-26-9

Depression era's social and political upheavals, such once-discrete subjects as history, geography and physics were amalgamated as social studies. To counter rural poverty and declining rural population, small local boards were consolidated into large school divisions.

Led by the Calgary public board, Alberta's urban school systems followed the provincial government along innovative pathways. Junior high schools (Grades 7–9) eased the curriculum and psychological transition between elementary grades and high-school years. Composite high schools brought academic, vocational and business education programs under one roof, allowing greater integration across the curriculum. Expanded opportunities for special-needs students helped schools better serve all the children of all the people.

Meanwhile, Alberta's teachers stood to benefit from the government's recognition of the Alberta Teachers' Association as their legitimate professional organization, with automatic membership for all teachers in the province's public and separate schools.

For many Alberta teachers, however, the decade of the 1930s meant financial cutbacks: reduced salaries, larger classes, fewer resources, less professional assistance from inspectors and consultants. Yet all across the province, in both rural and urban schools, these teachers rose to the challenges presented by the Great Depression, and continued to lead, encourage and inspire their students. Let's now meet Walter King, Tom Rodie, Catherine Barclay, Viviene Kennedy, William Shultz, Dorothy Tewksbury, Rev. John O'Halloran, Eileen Hughes, Amelia E. Bruce, Margaret Oak, and Alec Fernet.

A Veteran of Vimy Ridge

by Norma Sharpe

Walter King
Redcliff School, Redcliff

I was born and raised in Redcliff, once a boomtown nicknamed "Smokeless Pittsburgh"—an area described by Rudyard Kipling as "having all hell for a basement." It was comprised of Europeans (largely British) and Americans. Among them were businessmen, skilled tradesmen and labourers—all with great expectations. Alas, following the First World War, the investment money dried up and the manufacturing plants closed, as a result of bankruptcy or unexplained fires, which resulted in scarce financial resources for education.

As students, we never knew what resources were lacking when Walter King was appointed principal from 1930 to 1942. It was not until I reached high school that I fully recognised Mr. King's many skills in teaching and his overall contribution to my education.

Shakespeare came to life due to his theatrical talents—he had been a member of the famous *Dumbells* during the First

Canadian National Vimy Memorial.
Courtesy: Norma Sharpe

World War. The close of class found each of us sitting on the edge of our seats barely able to contain ourselves until the to-be-continued portion for the next

31

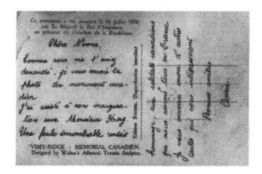

Postcard from Annie Duquesne

Lit class. He would voice each character—it simulated radio drama.

It was to our great advantage that Mr. King was fluent in French. At one point in the final course, he invited the class to his home for supper—the catch being, you could only speak in French. At times the crunch of celery was the only sound at the table! I became a pen pal of a family friend in France of Mr. King, one Annie Duquesne with whom I corresponded until the Second World War interrupted.

In history, current affairs were kept up-to-date on events leading up to the war and, because Mr. King was a veteran of Vimy Ridge, he was invited to attend the unveiling of the Vimy War Memorial in France. This provided an opportunity for us to learn firsthand details of European politics. I have a postcard of the memorial from my French correspondent, Annie (a member of the French underground during the Second World War), whom Mr. King was able to visit.

Physical education was encouraged by Mr. King. We played baseball, basketball, volleyball and in winter, with stones we collected according to shape and weight, we curled outdoors. In summer, he taught us how to make pyramid displays and perform athletic endeavours required in racing, jumping, throwing and general athletics—all this without formal equipment—no funds existed for such frivolities. Discipline was never a problem at recess. Should a couple of young fellows have a dispute, Mr. King would invite them to put on the boxing gloves during the next physical education class.

Music and drama were always in full swing; the Regional Music and Drama Festivals awarding many medals to Redcliff School participants. Lacking musical instruments, save a lonely piano, we placed waxed paper over combs to produce melodic sounds, the most expensive instrument being a Kazoo. In drama class, we constructed miniature Globe Theatres out of cardboard and learned how to properly apply stage make-up.

Domestic science, as such, was not available, but Mr. King arranged for sewing classes which included learning various embroidery stitches and how to use a treadle sewing machine. As a project, I completed an embroidered blouse.

I recall assembling a book of "styles" where I drew figures and glued material to them for each design.

Teaching health was unheard of because some parents questioned the whole notion. Mr. King, however, taught the boys and girls separately, probably as a concession to certain parents.

Most importantly, however, the highest academic standard of learning was never neglected. The graduating students always received honours in provincial academic exams.

Social life was introduced in the final year. At Christmas we enjoyed an evening of games and entertainment followed by dancing in the local "Cliff Hall". I was so proud when my father led me around the floor in my first attempt to waltz.

The fact my brother, Buzz Osgood, while in high school, was chosen the most outstanding cadet on parade by Brigadier Pearkes, was really a credit to Mr. King's training of these young, soon-to-be soldiers in the Second World War.

Recently, I attended a funeral of a former resident of Redcliff, Dan Jensen. I was impressed to note that his children, in the eulogy, stated that Mr. King, the high school principal, influenced and inspired Dan, a Danish immigrant, to overcome his language challenge to graduate and eventually become a teacher himself.

Despite the sparse funds available during the Depression in a town of 1,000 people, it is incredible that one dedicated and talented teacher had the resourcefulness to provide such broad and rich instruction to his students.

An Early Start on the Metric System
by Elizabeth Rodie

Tom Rodie
Delayed District School, Manyberries

Captain T.E. Rodie and daughter Edith, 1939.
Courtesy: Edith Rodie

I think it was in the early 1930s. We lived well in a nice house in Lethbridge but because we became part of the Dirty Thirties, we relocated to a farmhouse outside of the town of Manyberries—the Delayed District to be exact.

To describe that location would be to repeat the humorous contents of the television ad: "I walked four miles to school in 40 below weather"—it was absolutely true. I love that ad.

The teacher taught all grades in a one-room schoolhouse. Because I was the only one in my grade, I was moved up to a class where there was another student. I remember the teacher saying "You will skip and miss out on learning fractions and jump into learning the decimal system, but that won't hurt you and the day will come when the decimal system will replace fractions."

How clever he was! And what foresight he had! How grateful I was because it later put me in a position of being ahead of my time which is always advantageous. Although there were times I didn't know what others were doing with those fractions, I could do my figuring another way and to me it seemed less complicated. Also, I was always a little ahead of others even before the predicted change came.

There were many circumstances later on where this helped me and I felt inspired that this early start in the metric system could have such an effect. I often recall the day the teacher said those words to me and I picture him standing behind the centered pot-belly coal stove which he had started by arriving much earlier, in order to thaw out the schoolhouse prior to the arrival of the other students. And that would be after walking with me, Edith, the daughter of the schoolteacher, Mr. Tom Rodie, the four miles to school in 40 below.

And by the way, that was Fahrenheit!—in two foot snowdrifts!—in blizzards!

1 mile = 1.609 kilometres
1 foot = 0.3048 metres
-40 F = -40 C

A Beacon of Light

by Dorothy Gowen

Catherine Barclay
East Calgary High School, Calgary

Without having to give it a second thought, my favourite teacher was Miss E. Catherine Barclay. She was my French and English teacher for two years at East Calgary High School, during the last two years that the school functioned as a senior high school.

The English classes must have given her untold hours of work that could only be called drudgery. Every piece of paper we handed in for an assignment was carefully scrutinized. If a comma was out of place, or omitted, that mistake had to be corrected by us and returned to her for approval. To this day I never write a letter that her teaching doesn't come into my mind. She also arranged that we all have opportunities to deliver speeches to our fellow students. Many of us did not welcome this, but in later life came to realize its value. In addition, she initiated exchanges of letters between her students and overseas students; one of these has lasted over fifty years in my case.

My ability in French was minimal, and those classes were not very pleasant for me. She persuaded us to take part in a contest to find a winner who would receive a scholarship to attend a summer school course in the province of Quebec. Her wish was to make French more widespread in Canada.

I think the reason she became such a beacon of light for me was that she became a friend as well as a teacher. She encouraged me to join the Canadian Youth Hostel Association—an association that she brought to North America from its country of origin, Germany. She would take a few of us into the countryside around Calgary to help establish hostels where we could spend the night after hiking all day. This was a very new idea in 1933, when the first hostel in North America was founded at Bragg Creek by Miss Barclay and her sister Mary, along with the help of several of their friends. Our parents also deserve credit for agreeing to let us do this. We were only 14 and 15 years old, but such was Miss Barclay's influence that several of us were on hostel trips that gave us a taste of nature that left us longing for more.

Besides hostelling, she led a drama club at the school, because she felt the theatre was a worthwhile area for developing character. She gave her Friday evenings to lead the club. She had a remarkable ability to spot our strengths, put us in charge of an area where she felt we'd succeed, and then bow out of that particular project. She imparted to us a complete confidence that we would not fail her requests, and consequently we worked, researched, poured over library books, and went for advice to people in the area to get help. I don't think anyone in the club ever did let her down.

When she announced one spring that she was going to be in France during the next school term the dismay we felt was very near to hysteria, because the drama club meant so much to us. When she saw how emotionally involved we were she helped us organize a play-reading group which would meet in each other's homes on Friday nights. She gave us lists of plays to read and kept in touch by mail during the year she was away.

This outstanding woman expanded our horizons to cover the world, and helped us develop skills and confidence that I, for one, feel would have been unknown was it not for her.

Miss Kennedy and the Twins

by Frances (Wiethold) Booker and Ferdi (Wiethold) Neuman

Viviene Kennedy
Red Star Rural School, southeast of Fairview

In 1933 at the Red Star Rural School near Fairview in northern Alberta on the first day of another dreaded school year, two gangly and bespectacled girls stumbled their way to the back of the class, which was in every way their accustomed place. Beside the desk stood the tall, blond and smiling teacher. She faced thirty-six children in eight grades, at least 80 percent of who were struggling with English as a second language. Miss Viviene Kennedy knew she was in for a tough year. How could she smile so warmly?

After the first few days, she rearranged the seating. The twins were asked to move to the front seat in their respective rows. MAGIC! Now they could see the writing on the blackboard. Miss Kennedy had also noticed that their glasses did not appear to help them very much. The girls admitted that they had worn these glasses since before they had started school. No wonder the glasses looked too small. Something must be done about that. Miss Kennedy walked the two miles to their home to tell their father that new glasses were essential. Then she walked the two miles back to the teacherage. The glasses arrived in due course. School became a great deal more attractive.

The school was not supplied with artificial light of any kind; therefore the school day was shortened by one-half hour morning and afternoon from early November to mid-February further limiting the instructional time available. Supplies were very few and what was called the "Library" was, in fact, a single shelf with thirteen books for eight grades. There was no library in the community. At Miss Kennedy's request, the University of Alberta Extension Library sent a large trunk full of books every September while she remained at Red Star School. These trunks contained adult as well as children's books. Children were encouraged not only to read, but to encourage their older siblings and parents to do so as well.

Radios were still rare in the community. A few of the older boys would be invited to visit her in the teacherage at noon to hear the daily grain price report on her radio. They then took this important information home to their fathers. This was much appreciated.

When the school inspector arrived, Miss Kennedy had a plan. She pointed out to him that most of the twelve students in Grades 6, 7 and 8 would reach school-leaving age long before finishing Grade 8. Might she "please" push these students as hard as possible in the hope of completing as much as possible of the work of three years in two years? The inspector agreed. In June 1935 the four survivors, of the original twelve, wrote their Alberta departmental examinations with good results.

This spirit of faith in the students' abilities and encouragement to achieve carefully set goals, applied not only to the higher grades but to all the students. Her insistence on correct grammar and pronunciation was noticeable in the community for years. There was a distinct difference in the ability to clearly communicate between the "before and after Kennedy" citizens.

Miss Kennedy reprimanded when it was called for, but would soon be encouraging the student again. That horrible strap rarely came out of its drawer and even less often was it used. Older students learned what kindness and responsibility were about, when they helped the littlest ones. Miss Kennedy made clear to all students the value of her strong belief in honesty, responsibility and concern for fellow students. She helped them all.

After seventy years it is difficult to recall individual moments, but our school days changed dramatically. Now the students faced each day with anticipation and confidence. School was a joy. Having finished Grade 8, the twins had a keen desire for more education, which led them through high school and further training toward successful careers.

Miss Kennedy never stopped smiling. Some of her students kept in touch for many years. She is remembered with respect, gratitude and affection—especially by us, the twins.

Thank You, Wash

by Arthur Henry Rosenau

William Albert Shultz
Youngstown High School, Youngstown

As a youth growing up on the prairies, I encountered many fine teachers, both men and women. One who stands out in my memory was Mr. W.A. Shultz. School kids in those days had a nickname for things and people. In our private conversation we never referred to him as Mr. Shultz or the principal, but we affectionately called him "Wash", from the four letters of his name.

At the age of 14, having passed my provincial exams, I entered Youngstown High in 1934. I came under his tutorship for only one year. Wash, at 28 years old was so enthused with his work that I'm sure his enthusiasm rubbed off on us.

The Dust Bowl years and the Great Depression of the 1930s had decimated our school population. Farmers had gone bankrupt and left, merchants had closed their stores and most people had left the area. Mr. Shultz was teaching some twenty to thirty students, Grades 9 to 12, in all subjects as well as being principal. I don't know how he did it, but he managed all his various duties in a very systematic and organized fashion.

He was a fabulous teacher. Ancient history could have been terribly boring to a young teenager, but Mr. Shultz made it alive and interesting. He was a masterful artist with white and coloured chalk. He portrayed the Pharaohs of Egypt sailing up and down the Nile surveying their ancient empires. Then he showed the thousands of slaves pulling those huge twenty to thirty ton slabs of rock to the top of those magnificent pyramids; truly a fascinating sight.

He also imparted to his students some of his love for literature. Many of us learned more poems by memory in that year than in all of our lives. Many of these poems, like the *Ancient Mariner*, were quite lengthy. Even new subjects like Algebra 1 became easy—he used so many ways to explain a new and difficult concept that even the dullest student could understand.

He taught all subjects in four grades to scholars ranging in age from 13 to 24 years. Let me explain. A young man, Clarence Mellom, in the 1920s had quit high school to get a job and earn a fortune in life. He lost his job in the Great Depression and decided to come back and finish his education. Clarence came back to Grade 11, to the taunts and the teasing of all us younger kids. He graduated from high school and went on to become a teacher because of the encouragement of Mr. Shultz.

In spite of his many duties, Mr. Shultz found time to conduct a literary society one evening each week at the school. He encouraged us to write poems and stories and then recite them to the assembled group. I recall one evening in particular. I had written a poem of ten lines and I was called to the front to recite it. As I stood up to speak I saw the sea of faces before me and my mind went blank. I couldn't remember a single word. I beat a hasty retreat to my seat, embarrassed and ashamed. Mr. Shultz came and patted me on the shoulder and said, "Never mind Arthur, the words will come back to you," and they did. With his help and encouragement I was able to get up later and present my poem and receive the applause of all my fellow students. Such was the tact, the care, and the understanding of this great teacher. In spite of all his frustrations having so many subjects to teach to such a diverse group of students, I never saw him lose his composure.

As a child I had always intended to follow in my father's footsteps and become a railroad engineer. However it was the fine example of this "master teacher", Mr. W.A. Shultz, who encouraged me to follow a nobler and more rewarding profession and become a teacher. I pay tribute to him with these words: Thank you, Wash, for your powerful influence on my life.

Children Wanted to Behave

by Jim Foster

Dorothy Tewksbury
Lonely Trail School, Oyen

In the mid-1930s, a young lady, aged 18 or 19, arrived from Calgary to teach at the Lonely Trail School: a one-room school situated about half way between Oyen and Acadia Valley.

The school housed students from Grades 1 to 10; and provided space for the teacher to help students taking Grade 11 and 12 courses by correspondence. What a huge challenge for young Dorothy Tewksbury! She acted as a mother and big sister to many of the students and made each of them feel special. Besides all the teaching duties, a teacher at that time was also expected to be a practical nurse, attending to all the cuts, bruises and nosebleeds. Soon after her arrival, she was called on to attend to a young student who had suffered a serious accident when run over by a horse. His arm was shattered and he went into convulsions. The nearest phone was over a mile away and the doctor was thirty miles away. Miss Tewksbury dealt with the situation with calmness and maturity until the doctor finally arrived and took the poor boy to the hospital.

Miss Tewksbury was boarded at a local farm and rode horseback two miles to school, winter and summer. Upon arrival at school, Miss Tewksbury not only made certain that all the students learned what they needed to, she planned and organized many extra activities that greatly affected the lives of her students. She organized games at noon and recess, planned and put on Christmas concerts, and directed plays and skits. At her own expense, she supplied guitars to teach lessons in Spanish after school and on Saturdays. One student's talent was unleashed and in later years he did some recording.

Children wanted to behave for Miss Tewksbury, who had a wonderful way with them and dealt very well with the few discipline problems I recall. One winter day, as Miss Tewksbury was bent over helping the girls make a snowman, one of the older boys hit her on the rear end with a hard snowball. The girls must have turned in the culprit. She never said a word to him but knew he was always the last one to enter the porch when school was called in. She was waiting inside beside the door and caught him full in the face with of couple of handfuls of ice and snow.

This amazing teacher also supplied skis for us to use. I don't know how she managed to buy these for us with very poor pay and often having to wait months to get it. She must have spent nearly all her wages on these goodies for us. She also made sure each student had entries prepared for the annual School Fair in Oyen.

When Miss Tewksbury completed her teaching stint at Lonely Trail, she invited all the boys from the school to the Calgary Stampede. Imagine the thrill for prairie boys who had never seen a city! Four of us were able to come up with the train fare. She met the train, took us to her parents' home, where we all slept. She drove us all over the city to see the sights and took us to a day at the Stampede. We only had to pay for a few treats.

During the Second World War, when I was stationed in Halifax, I found out Dorothy was also stationed there with the Air Force (WD). I was delighted to meet up with her. Unfortunately, I was broke as usual and, once again, Miss Tewksbury treated me, this time to lunch and a show. She was still the teacher and a very giving soul.

I am convinced that every pupil at that school would agree that she was the best and most respected teacher they ever had.

I dedicate this to the most wonderful teacher and a grand lady, Miss Dorothy Tewksbury.

He Decided on a Plan for Me

by Cecile Dumas

Rev. John O'Halloran
Theresetta Separate School, Castor

John J. O'Halloran was born of Irish parents in Glasgow, Scotland, a combination that probably influenced his distinctive character. His wit and humour were Irish, but his stern and demanding nature as a teacher reflected his Jesuit training in Scotland.

In 1912, he responded to Canadian Pacific Railway advertisements and was hired as a bookkeeper for $275.00 a year, twice as much as he would have made in Scotland. During the First World War, he found himself in the Canadian Army Medical Corps.

After the war, feeling a call to the priesthood, he entered a seminary and was ordained after six years of study. In 1925 he was sent to Castor where he remained for forty-two years. There, besides presiding over his parishioners, taking an interest in the politics of the town, the province, and Canada, he was proudest of his involvement in education.

He was instrumental in establishing Theresetta School in Castor. An old church and disused bank building were transformed into a school. In the 30s, he argued before the school board that a final high school year should be added to the curriculum. Theresetta Separate School became fully accredited with Grade 12, just like city schools.

It was in 1934 that my mother had me enrolled in Theresetta for Grade 10. Father O'Halloran taught his Grade 12 mathematics upstairs. Those of us in the downstairs classroom often heard loud rapping on the table above, setting off a large "bong" from the old disused clock on the downstairs wall. We were regularly regaled by the Grade 12s of incidents that occurred upstairs. His reputation as a demanding teacher was established.

In 1936, six of us graduated to the classroom upstairs. Father O'Halloran stood before us, his cassock green with age and side pockets in need of mending. Holding a pointer, he sternly looked at each one of us. He turned toward the blackboard and started writing. The letters formed at the beginning were readable but the sentence gradually deteriorated into a straight line. He gazed at us saying, "That's clear isn't it?" We didn't dare say no and answered, "Yes Father." He burst into chuckles and proceeded to teach the concept. Between mathematical projects he interspersed anecdotes, jokes, and even burst out indignantly against some government policy. He held our attention.

That year, he decided that a Theresetta student would get the Lieutenant-Governor's award. In previous years, the public school in Castor had won it. Every Saturday, he tutored another girl and me in mathematics. We duly wrote our departmental exams. When the results came out, she was one point ahead of me and she won the award to the honour of Theresetta.

I thought that was the end of my education. My father was of the old European school and felt professions were not for girls—they only ended up getting married. My mother held the opposite view. I heard loud arguments over the issue. In fairness to my father, it was during the Depression.

Even though he was probably not aware of the conflict, Father O'Halloran settled it. He made the thirty mile trip to the farm to advise my parents that he had decided on a plan for me. I was to go to Camrose Normal School. He knew of a good family in town who would room and board me. He would mail me $20.00 a month of which $18.00 would go for room and board and the remaining $2.00 could be my spending money. Who could refuse that?

Consequently, in 1937–38, I found myself attending Camrose Normal School, one of seventy-nine girls and nineteen boys, the last year it was open. There we were trained to manage eight grades in one room, balance attendance records, and be creative with any materials at hand in those depression years. It launched many a career in country schools and even graded city schools.

I suspect Father O'Halloran helped others establish themselves in professions. Many graduates from Theresetta found a calling in the one-room schools prevalent in Alberta. Whenever former students of the school meet, they usually reminisce in amusement but end up in admiration of that extraordinary teacher, Father O'Halloran.

She Made Every Day Neat

by Robert Breakell

Eileen (Hughes) McRae
Montreal Street School, Medicine Hat

Robert B. Breakell—front and centre!
Courtesy: Robert Breakell

I grew up in a C.P.R. railroad family. It was September 1938 and we were living in Medicine Hat. My dad was upset when he enrolled me in Grade 1 at Montreal Street School because he had to buy and produce a birth certificate to prove my date of birth. My teacher was Miss Eileen Hughes—all the lady teachers were single which must have been the rules of the day.

Miss Hughes made every day neat. To start the day, the class would recite the Lord's Prayer aloud standing up by our desks; then we would all come to attention and sing the national anthem, *God Save The King*. Then we would begin to learn the alphabet. Five or six of the class got to go to the blackboard and print with chalk the capital letter "A" and the small "a". Those not at the blackboard would print out the letters at their desks with pencil on paper. Around 10:30 a.m. and 2:30 p.m. the bell would ring in the halls and everyone went out to the school yard for a ten-minute recess. After recess, Miss Hughes started out with our numbers the same way she did with the alphabet. Before anyone could believe it, the school bell rang and it was now noon hour.

Everyone went home for lunch. School was back in at 1:00 p.m. Miss Hughes would read one chapter each day from books like *The Wizard of Oz*. The afternoon passed very quickly with choir singing, arts and crafts, and sometimes spelling or arithmetic quizzes. We sang *We will hang our washing on the Seigfried line* in the music festival held at the Alexander High School—I was in the front row.

The Second World War brought the King, Queen and Princesses to Medicine Hat in May 1939 on the C.P.R. special train. All the schools got to line up on North Railway Street and the royal party waved to us.

My first year of school was the best and I was so happy I passed. One of my friends didn't and I felt bad for him.

Later, when I was graduating from Grade 12, we were allowed to invite our parents and one other. I took my mom and dad and Miss Hughes. She told me she was thrilled to be asked because it was the first graduation she had been invited to by one of her students.

Mrs. (Hughes) McRae certainly left her mark in Medicine Hat. I have no idea how many students she taught, but her skills in music, forming choirs, provided wonderful entertainment. Medicine Hat will remember her untold hours of community service.

The Tall Lady in the Yellow Smock

by David S. Thomson

Amelia E. Bruce
Connaught School, Calgary

David's Grade 5 report card.
Courtesy: David Thomson

Miss A.E. Bruce was my most memorable teacher. This was a no-brainer. She was my Grade 5 teacher at Connaught School in Calgary, 1938–1939. It was positively the best thing that ever happened to me. This was the beginning of a beautiful year in my otherwise drab life.

It was the late days of the Great Depression. I had lost my father in 1934. My mother and I were just getting by, and school was just so-so. It was like a light had broken through for me. I remember this tall lady in the yellow smock. Her hair was brown and cut short, and she carried herself with great dignity.

She awakened a desire for learning that lay below the surface of my life. I will always remember her for the kindness and thoughtfulness she brought into my life and all the students. A fellow student once stated, "I was a real reprobate in school except for the year in her class, because I did not want to upset her." I think that is a real tribute.

Miss Bruce instilled in me a love of reading. She read a great variety of classic stories to the class, such as *Black Beauty, The Yearling, The Count of Monte Cristo, King Arthur* and *Jean Val Jean*, about the man who stole a loaf of bread to feed his family and was sent to jail. This is when I realized in my young mind that reading could open many doors. I started going to the Central Park Library on a regular basis to hear the Saturday morning stories told by Miss Georgina Thomson and to pick up my books.

As my report card shows I did improve in many areas. Solving math problems was one of my weaknesses. Miss Bruce had a very tight system. Every Thursday morning we had a spelling test; Thursday afternoon it was an accuracy test—adding, subtracting, multiplying and dividing; Friday morning was problem solving. This was the bane of my existence, but this beautiful, patient lady persevered and I progressed, all be it slowly.

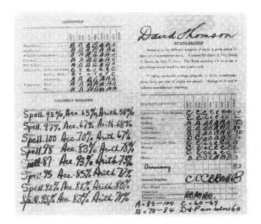

Signs of improvement. *Courtesy: David Thomson*

Social studies was also a highlight of the year. The *Calgary Herald* supplied large scrap books. We did most of our social studies in these large books. We made maps, drew pictures and learned all about early explorers like Champlain and the Order of the Good Time in Nova Scotia at Port Royal. I visited there a few years ago and remembered her story of this historic event. Miss Bruce made history come alive for us. Miss Bruce awarded us for having a good scholastic week by relating stories of her experiences in China prior to the war.

Miss Bruce awakened in me a desire to learn. I'm sure she touched the lives of every student she taught. When I became a teacher my hope was to inspire students the way she had done. She left me with a legacy of dreams.

She Served Us Hot Soup and Cocoa for Lunch

by Florence Vaile Anderson

Margaret Oak
Plateau School, Elnora

Margaret Oak (left rear) and her class (Florence – 2nd row on the right). Plateau School 1938–1939; *Courtesy: Florence Anderson*

My most memorable teacher was a young woman from Elnora, Alberta who came to teach at our school in September 1938. Her name was Miss Margaret Oak and the school was named Plateau. Our school sat on a small knoll in a prairie pasture in southern Alberta. It was the beginning of the end of one-room country schools.

Miss Oak lived in the teacherage, a little house beside the school. Conditions were very primitive with no indoor plumbing, electricity or transportation. Miss Oak depended a great deal on our parents for groceries, water and other necessities living alone and so far away from town. Her only company was her younger brother who lived with her, and she taught him Grade 7.

Although there were not many students going to Plateau, Miss Oak still had to teach Grades 1 to 9. She was a good and dedicated teacher who rewarded students who worked hard. I remember receiving a copy of *The Little Lame Prince* as a prize for attaining high marks on my report card!

During the cold winter months at recess she would go to the teacherage to prepare soup with milk and tomatoes. At noon she would bring it over to the school and serve us hot soup and cocoa. I always hated my cold sandwiches for lunch and the warm, steaming treats tasted so good!

Miss Oak baked special cakes for birthdays, iced with designs that made the top look like a crocheted doily. At the end of the day on the Friday closest to our birthdays she cut the beautiful cakes into different shaped pieces. Sometimes we would find wrapped nickels or treasures in our slice of cake.

We had a Junior Red Cross Club in our school. During the club meetings I learned to knit, do fancy embroidery stitches and hand-sew. She taught my sister, Eileen, to dance the Irish jig. She showed the boys how to paint pictures on glass and do other crafts.

At the end of the 1938–1939 term, the district decided to close our little school. Miss Oak and her two older brothers, who had come to help her move, planned an outdoor family night. They invited all of us and our parents. The Oaks built a small bonfire for us. In those days, bonfires had to be small because the land was so dry during the ten years of drought. I had never been around a campfire. Miss Oak and her brothers entertained us with their beautiful singing. We sang and played games in the school yard until late in the evening while the adults visited.

On a clear, starry June night, Miss Oak and her students bid goodbye to our small one-room prairie school.

A Door Opens
by Georgie Collins

Alec Fernet
Edson Trail School, near Debolt

September of 1939 was a time of great expectations. Word was that we were to have—for the very first time—a "man" teacher. I felt a twinge of angst and a great deal of uncertainty. In a home where the father figure was so dominant, I was sure there would be little softness in his heart. I had him pegged as somewhat like the school masters in the works of Charles Dickens—a long, narrow face and an ever present cane. Of course he would wear black.

Mr. Fernet disappointed me in the very nicest kind of way. He was slender and tall—with a ready smile. His dress pants and shirt were in tans and brown and topped with a cardigan; he gave us a cheery "good morning" and then, as had all the other teachers before him, he started with the grade ones and worked his way up to the grade nines asking, "What is your name? What would you like to become?" My answer was not tentative, "I'm going to be an actress!" The giggles started but were soon under control as Mr. Fernet replied "I think you would be a very good actress." He won my heart forever.

It was May 1940 and I was nearing my fifteenth birthday. Soon it would be time for the school year to end and Mr. Fernet would be walking out of my life. A door would be closing but one of the biggest doors in my life would be given a nudge open. In April of that year, the good teacher had approached my parents about the possibility of entering me in a speech festival to be held in the town. They had agreed and all plans were made. I spent time in my lunch hours and after school working with my mentor on the chosen festival piece, *The Parable of the Good Samaritan*. I memorized it quickly and without difficulty, but soon learned there would be more expected of me than simple memorization. I had to learn to "tell the story". Did I understand it? Could I manage to lift the words off the page and make them my own? It was the basis of everything I would one day learn was necessary to become an actress.

52

May 16th came and I shook with the excitement of it all. My mother had sent to the catalogue and bought me a print dress with puffy sleeves and a Peter Pan collar. I thought it was lovely. She curled my fine and spindly hair. Then my father took me to the grocery store where the mail truck and Mr. Fernet waited. This truck went in twice weekly for supplies and was the only source of transportation. We sat in the big back box of the truck and no plane or car or train has ever taken me on a happier journey.

We arrived at the hall, which was sitting close to a quaint, brick, Anglican church nestled in some trees. As we walked in the door my heart sank. I was desolate. Rows of girls sat in the seats and turned to look as we came in. They all wore little pleated skirts and shirts with smart blazers or else exquisite dress-es, the like of which I'd never seen. My dress was suddenly "wrong"—my hair—my height (I was too tall). I was aware of how I looked for the first time in my life, and I didn't stack up. I felt ugly. I looked up at Mr. Fernet and said, "I don't want to do this. I look awful!" He said, "I'm sorry! I'm sure you said you want-ed to be an actress. Let's just take a seat and when they call your name, if you go up, I'll be sitting here and when I nod you tell your story."

One by one they called names and the girls recited the parable. As I listened I understood why Mr. Fernet did not like the word "recite". I knew as I listened that I could get up and tell the story. I looked at his face—he smiled and nod-ded—and I told the story of *The Good Samaritan*—and won. I now knew for sure and true I would one day be an actress! I walked up to the front to receive my diploma and stood as tall as ever I could. I still have the framed certificate now aged and ragged from time.

It was late and I went to bed as soon as I got home. I would tell all the details to everyone tomorrow; but tonight I would fall asleep savouring the whole wonderful day. My little attic room became more precious now. My dream had suddenly become possible!

To a young girl called Georgina, who would one day become Georgie and who would go on to do well over a hundred stage productions and forty films; and who would share time and a scotch or two with Sir Laurence Olivier—Mr. Fernet has always been her very own patron saint of the theatre.

Chapter 3
Teachers of the 1940s

The Second World War influenced Alberta education in a myriad of ways. Many teachers left their schools for wartime service overseas; some would not return, like William Lay, killed in a bombing raid over Germany. Other teachers left for higher-paying jobs in war-related industries that mushroomed in the province's major cities. On the home classroom front, Alberta teachers inspired their young charges through patriotic literature and social studies classes, led rousing "hurrah-for-Britain" sing-songs, and encouraged students to buy war bonds and war-savings stamps to help finance Canada's military effort.

In this chapter, grateful students introduce us to those memorable teachers whose inspiration provided comfort and challenge through those difficult wartime years. Meet Bill Lay, Carl Carlson, Percy Page (a future Alberta lieutenant-governor), Robbie Robinson, Earl Buxton, Bill Allan, and Doug Johnson.

With peace in 1945, and the important Leduc oil bonanza two years later, the province entered a welcome period of social stability and economic prosperity. RCAF veteran Sidney Lindstedt (later a professor in the Faculty of Education, University of Calgary) takes us into the second half of the decade, along with fellow teachers Winston Churchill (of Calgary, not Britain), Sister Marie Luciana, Freda Sauter, June Crook and Alfred Howard.

The year 1945 also saw Alberta become the first province to transfer all responsibility for teacher education to its provincial university. The Edmonton Normal School merged with the Faculty of Education at the University of Alberta; the Calgary Normal School became the Calgary Branch of the U of A, and eventually the University of Calgary. In the not-too-distant future lay the goal of a university degree for all beginning teachers.

Wish Me Luck As You Wave Me Goodbye
by Gordon Littke

William Robert Lay
Annellen School, near Hythe

Annellen School, circa 1939. *Courtesy: Gordon Littke*

William Lay was known in the community as "Bill," but was Mr. Lay to the twenty-two farm children who attended Annellen School. Mr. Lay must have loved teaching, because he worked very hard to make learning fun. He was an actor and a talented musician, and gave the impression that teaching was spontaneous.

He brought a teddy bear as a prop for early reading classes. He named the bear "Snooky", added overalls, then a hammer, and had him doing farm chores. Blackboard words included "cow" and "feed" as well as "jump" and "run" from the *Jerry and Jane* reader. His book choice to read aloud for Grades 4 to 6 was *Winnie the Pooh*. Everyone tuned in for Mr. Lay's animation of Pooh, Owl and Eyore.

Christmas concerts were major events in rural Alberta. Teachers began preparing programs soon after starting the school term. Mr. Lay's concert sparkled with imagination and originality. The 1940 concert opened with the choir singing the original French version of *O' Canada* and *The Maple Leaf* in English. He scripted a play for three actors from O. Henry's story, *The Ransom of Red Chief*. The main pageant was Shakespeare's "The Seven Ages of Man", from *As You Like It*. Staging called for a reader and a choir, plus pantomime actors for each age. Mimes entered stage left, and slowly crossed the stage as the lines were read and as the choir sang an appropriate song. They exited stage right to rejoin the choir. Sixty-five years later, I can recall six of the seven songs:

Brahms' Lullaby Playmates (infant), *Oh! Johnny!* (youth), *Wish Me Luck As You Wave Me Goodbye* (soldier), *Silver Threads Among the Gold* (elderly), and *Swing Low, Sweet Chariot* (dotage).

Mr. Lay joined outdoor games during lunch hours. He filled the roles of mentor, coach or mediator, but was sometimes a participant. At softball, he took the pitcher's mound when batters were from the early grades, then became an umpire when older children were at bat. He made sure that rules were followed in all games.

Mr. Lay made school enjoyable, but expected specific levels of accomplishment from each person. He assigned work projects, and left no doubt that results were expected on time. Our library was about fifty books plus a world map, and most families received one or two weekly newspapers. We were expected to use these resources and to deliver our best efforts. He gave prompt marks and was enthusiastic in his praise of good work. He made us feel proud of our achievements.

William Robert Lay, circa 1943.
Courtesy: Gordon Littke

There were two of us in each of Grades 7 through 9. In mid-May, Mr. Lay announced a joint social studies project, a debate between two teams of three. He explained the rules of debate and gave us the topic: "Resolved, that Japan is a threat to British, French and American possessions in the Pacific." Obviously, neither team could discuss material or plan strategy inside the school without being overheard by opponents, so teams were given alternate days to work outside the schoolroom: the school porch in rainy weather, outdoors on nice days. Of course we played games while outdoors, but we recognized our obligation to Mr. Lay's trust and actually did productive school work. The debate was timely, less than six months before Pearl Harbor.

Just before the school year ended, an inspector visited Annellen. He monitored classes and then met privately with myself and two other students. He questioned me on social studies, mathematics and science topics. It developed that Mr. Lay had recommended that three of his twenty-two students should skip a grade and that none should fail. As a "rookie" teacher, his recommendations had to be validated by a school inspector. When my report card arrived, I was promoted from Grade 7 to Grade 9.

Mr. Lay left to enlist in the Canadian Army; later transferring to the RCAF where he became a Flying Officer by rank, serving as a navigator. He died in a bomber over Muenster, Germany at age 24, just forty-four days before the Second World War ended.

Stand Up and Take the War

by Hon. Nick Taylor

Carl Carlson
Sunnymeade School, Bow Island

It seems that I have been blessed with outstanding classroom teachers from Grade 1 on. Part of the reason was probably because in southern Alberta during the Depression, the outstanding teachers did not have the opportunity to move on to jobs that were more rewarding, at least money-wise.

Of the many, the one that sticks in my mind the most was Carl Carlson, my teacher in Grades 7 and 8. He taught six grades in a little one-room country schoolhouse called Sunnymeade, twelve miles out on the bald-headed prairie, southeast of Bow Island on the way to the U.S. border. Mr. Carlson lived with his wife, Jean and their baby, Gerry, in a two-room teacherage, 150 feet from the school, sharing the hand-dug cellar with a pair of grateful skunks.

Carl Carlson introduced me to two of the greatest loves of my life: the English poets and geography. As a youngster in 1941, too young to join up, my soul was kindled by poems like Byron's *Destruction of Sennacherib* and Kipling's *For All We have and Are*. I could almost see on an early prairie morn, the "Assyrian [coming] down like a wolf on the fold and their cohorts gleaming in purple and gold." Likewise Kipling's "Stand up and take the war, the Hun is at the gate," made me ache to be a foot taller and three years older.

Geography became my lifetime hobby, pushing me first to geology, and then travelling most of the world.

Later, when I took Grade 9 by correspondence, he used to drop in on his weekly trip to town to encourage me to keep at it, and occasionally helped me with a math problem.

I shall never forget him!

Why Settle For a Star

by Alice Roberts

J. Percy Page
McDougall Commercial High School, Edmonton

He was tall and handsome. His very stern demeanour let you know there was no fooling around in his classes. One foggy morning I arrived late for class. He met me at the door of his office (he was the PRINCIPAL). "Why are you late," he asked.

"I could not see the bus in the fog," I said.

"I once had to walk a mile to school," he said.

"I have just walked three miles," I said.

"Go to your class," he said. I was never late again, but after that exchange he remembered my name and used it.

Regardless of what subject he taught, he taught it with a passion. Mediocre work was never accepted. Everyone in the class was expected to do the best they could possibly do. No one ever failed to measure up to his expectations. "Why settle for a star when you could have the moon?" How often have I used that statement speaking to my own children!

He coached the most winning ladies' basketball team in the world (the Grads) and went on to become a Member of the Alberta Legislature and a Lieutenant Governor. Mr. J. Percy Page was a mentor, a leader and a gentleman and my favourite teacher.

He Gave Me a Slide Rule

by Harvey A. Buckmaster

George "Robbie" Robinson
Central Collegiate Institute, Calgary

Central Collegiate Institute (CCI) in Calgary, Alberta was an unusual high school because it accepted only eighty students from the many who applied for admission each year based on their Grade 9 provincial examination results. It had an outstanding reputation for preparing students for their Grade 12 senior matriculation examinations and university entrance because CCI had a distinguished and highly competent group of teachers, each of whom was memorable, but for me, George Robinson stood apart because he had the greatest impact on my life and career.

I first encountered him in Algebra I when I entered Grade 10 in the fall of 1943. Robbie, as he was affectionately referred to by his students, was a slight, not very tall man with grey, thinning hair and spoke with a quiet but firm voice. He employed a unique, individualized teaching methodology that was effective for both typical and gifted students.

Robbie had a lesson plan for each class in which he wrote the new material to be covered on the blackboards at the front of his classroom and the exercises for the students to solve using this new material were written on the blackboards on one side of the room. He would carefully explain the new material for about twenty minutes and then the students had the remaining thirty to work on these exercises. They were designed to take the typical student the remainder of the class period. However, those students who completed the exercises before the end of the class were encouraged to raise an arm. There was competition to be the first one finished. Robbie would come and inspect the student's work. If the solutions were correct, then he would take a pile of file cards on which were printed mathematical problems out of a pocket in the pale blue linen dust jacket that he always wore. He would carefully select an appropriate problem and give it to the student to solve. They were extremely challenging and I always found them great fun to tackle.

I recall that, during the first class I had from Robbie, he gave me a slide rule and suggested that I try to figure out how it worked. I had worked out how to multiply by the end of the class when I returned it to him. After school that day, I bicycled downtown to Osborne Stationary on 8th Avenue S.W. and purchased a slide rule. I still own this slide rule and it remains functional although the numbers and letters are well worn. The problem that I remember most clearly concerned Zeno's paradox with the hare and the tortoise. I puzzled over it until I learned about infinite series. Each exposed one to some new area or idea in mathematics.

Robbie was a talented mathematician who had abandoned a promising career in Scotland, and returned to Calgary to teach high school mathematics to support his parents. He could earn more money as a high school teacher than as a university professor in the 1920s. Hopefully, he had greater impact on the mathematical community by using his talents to teach at the high school level than as a lecturer in Scotland.

I am most indebted to him for introducing me to the world of mathematics. Robbie was truly a memorable teacher and the fact that I went on to do graduate work in mathematics attests to his influence on my life and career.

You're Just Beginning to Know Something

by Ruth (Gould) Miller

Earl Buxton
Garneau School and University High School, Edmonton

In September 1943, we giggly girls in a Grade 7 class at Garneau School were unanimous about one thing: our homeroom teacher, Earl Buxton, was handsome, a great teacher and fun. Even the boys were impressed, as he had been an Alberta amateur boxing champion, but they were not impressed by his car. Its age and infirmities were discussed and taken as proof that teachers' salaries were lousy.

The Second World War was raging and a competition was organized to see which home room could buy the most war bonds. Out of our babysitting and lawn mowing earnings, we each bought twenty-five cent stickers until we managed to complete a five dollar bond. Mr. Buxton divided us into teams, and on a side blackboard tracked our progress. Heading each team's column was a cartoon, and very good cartoons they were. His remarkable talent for drawing was very aptly used in more challenging situations.

On one such occasion, a fight broke out at the back of the room as a girl and boy whacked away with books, wrestled and screeched. Mr. Buxton walked in. What would he do? Send the scrappy pair to the principal's office? Impose detentions? A tongue-lashing? Without a word he strode to the front of the room and with a few deft strokes drew on the blackboard a club-toting caveman dragging a girl by the hair. A shame-faced peace descended.

With the end of war came rumours that the Commonwealth Air Training School had moved out of the former normal school (now Corbett Hall), and we would be attending the new University High School located in the north wing. Wonder of wonders, Mr. Buxton would move there with us, and he would still be mentoring us in math, physics and English. His zest for life, kind and gentle nature, tolerance, sense of humour, and public speaking ability would, over time, help to mould many lives.

English was his special interest and with him we would continue discovering the excitement of English literature. In one instance, during Grade 12, Mr. Buxton declared a "Puzzle Poems Week," during which we explored allusions, topical references, seeming obscurities and other details to seek out meaning and relevance.

Another of his impressive projects was a style analysis program which required us to write, to critique each other's work, and then write more—always with his guidance and encouragement. I later learned that his doctoral dissertation at Stanford University explored how people learn to write well. Mr. Buxton's focus was always on the use of language, the expression of meaning and emotion, and he believed understanding of grammar should develop through this experience. Thus, near the end of Grade 12 he announced, "This is not the best way to learn grammar, but the departmental exams are coming and they will test you on the rules, so here goes." He filled blackboard after blackboard with grammatical lore, explaining as he went, preparing us for the inevitable.

We always knew that Mr. Buxton was fond of us and fair to us, and therefore we understood and accepted a comment he made just before graduation. "You have progressed from students who knew everything to the realization that you're just beginning to know something."

This marvellous teacher eventually became a professor in the Faculty of Education, at the University of Alberta, Calgary Branch. When I last saw him, he still remembered me as "the little red head in the third row."

It's More Important to Teach Young People

by Ralph Miller

William K. Allan
Western Canada High School, Calgary

My first class with Mr. Allan was in September 1945, Grade 10, at Western Canada High School. One could not be interested in amateur radio, or even just hang around with a few radio "hams" in those days without becoming aware of W.K. Allan. In class he wore a white lab coat which, along with an unruly fringe of black hair around a substantial bald spot, produced a considerable semblance of mad professor. The intensity of his teaching reinforced this semblance, as he diagrammed and explained some of the marvellous instruments which were coming into the public realm after the Second World War. If some students were baffled by these detailed explanations they never showed it, and discipline was never a problem. Very simply, it was much too fascinating just watching Mr. Allan working at full speed.

Bill Allan was a virtuoso at the blackboard, outlining complex objects freehand while keeping all parts in proportion and describing their functions and relations. He introduced us to such entities as the magnetron, where a combination of crossed electrical and magnetic fields, produce the high-powered oscillations at microwave frequencies necessary for radar. Bill gave us many such wonderful instances of how things work, and he also had many practical suggestions. Back in those days of "knob and tube" wiring and fuse boxes, his routine for finding short circuits was beautiful. Put a low wattage bulb in place of the blown fuse, then go about the house unplugging lamps and appliances and jiggling wires. When the light goes out, you have found the short circuit.

Despite all his diagrams and theory, Bill Allan was not teaching physics, but rather, electrical shop, and his classes were not filled with academically-oriented students. Even so, out of his classes came students who would score among the highest marks in physics.

Bill elegantly blended the practical and theoretical and fascinated even the least imaginative students with an array of equipment—built by him. Literally towering above the other equipment was a Tesla coil, a slender, wire-wrapped cylinder, appropriately capped with a metal sphere, from which could be drawn sparks arcing over a distance of seven or eight inches. This coil propagated hundreds of thousands of volts, and in order to make it Bill had constructed a condenser of immense capacity which was discharged across a spark gap to produce high frequency electrical current to energize the few and heavy primary windings of the Tesla coil. Bill, of course, had also wound the thousand plus turns of wire on the secondary coil and had calculated the values for all the components. Nowadays, components for Tesla coils are advertised on the internet, but W.K. Allan was five decades ahead of them.

One of the joys of taking a shop course was building something of your own, and Bill had an arrangement with Taylor, Pearson and Carson—then the largest radio equipment dealers in Calgary—where his students could get parts at close to wholesale prices. Thus it was that I built a combination radio and record player and an electronic timer for use in photographic processing.

There was much more to Bill Allan than theory and technique, for he was a thoughtful and highly principled man who embodied all that is best in the ideals of craftsmanship. Moreover, his interests were wide so that pausing after class, or better yet, coming round after school to ask a question, could lead to fascinating conversations. And it was he who encouraged me to read more history and to dig into books such as *Science for the Citizen* and *Prodigal Genius*.

One glimpse of Bill Allan's background and attitude was provided by Norman Pickard, a science teacher and colleague of mine at Crescent Heights High School. He said that Bill had spent some time in research, and gave this reason for leaving: "There are other guys who can do research, and it's more important to teach young people."

I shall be forever grateful to W.K. Allan, for even though I did not choose to pursue science at university, he opened vistas and laid the foundations of understanding which have served me well over many years.

He Changed My Musical Tastes for the Better

by Mary (Guterson) Campbell

Doug Johnson
Drumheller Central School, Drumheller

Growing up in the coal mining town of Drumheller in the 1940s, I attended Drumheller Central School. I was in Grade 6 and had a wonderful music teacher by the name of Mr. Doug Johnson. He changed my musical tastes for the better and gave me a better appreciation for classical music.

Music period was held in the old basement of the school in a small, crowded room and the smell of the old coal stoker and lots of black coal dust was everywhere.

Mr. Johnson was a very fashionable and impeccable dresser—white shirt, tie, blue, pressed suits and highly polished black shoes. He also played the piano and his hands and finger nails were so clean. Most of our fathers were hard-working men at jobs that clean nails and hands were not the norm.

Central School, Drumheller, circa 1940s.
Courtesy: Town of Drumheller Archives

He would put movies on the old projector that flickered or records on the phonograph. It was our lesson to identify the song, orchestra and name the various instruments that we had heard. Sometimes we would have to listen to an opera and you can imagine all the groans and comments, especially from the boys. He encouraged and requested those pupils who played any instruments to bring them to school and play for the class. He was never critical of any pupil who made a mistake or didn't play very well. I remember that after two years of piano lessons I could master only chop sticks.

I come from a large family of eleven, and had sisters who played the piano, but I didn't inherit their talent. I like to sing but only for my own enjoyment. Mr. Johnson encouraged me to enjoy classical music and to this day I love it and have a good collection of classical records, tapes and CDs. I also enjoy going to the Calgary opera productions.

I have to say that the influence of Mr. Johnson and his love of good music truly did change my musical tastes for the better, to enjoy and appreciate the talents of good artists, singers and composers and their resulting beautiful music.

Four-feet, Twenty-seven Inches Tall

by Margaret (Feyrer) Clarke and Norma (Stephenson) Lendrum

Sidney A. Lindstedt
Cayley School, Cayley

"I know you are all wondering how tall I am. Well, I am four-feet, twenty-seven inches." And so, Sidney A. Lindstedt entered the lives of the high school students of Cayley School, in the spring of 1945. Resplendent in his Royal Canadian Air Force dress blue, we were awestruck. Returning immediately after his discharge, he soon became the most respected and admired teacher we had ever had. Truly head and shoulders above all other teachers—our most memorable teacher.

Cayley High School class of '49. Sidney Lindstedt (left rear). Norma (2nd along left wall). Margaret (front – 2nd from left). *Courtesy: Margaret Clarke*

In the Cayley school Grades 7 to 12 were accommodated in two rooms, which meant that two teachers had to teach all subjects—the departmental exam subjects for Grades 9 and 12 and everything else. Many talents were needed and Mr Lindstedt rose to the challenge. Math and sciences were his fields, but when some of us voted for Latin he bravely took it on and did a good job. He made *Macbeth* come frighteningly alive. Some wanted drama and he inspired us to an ambitious production of *Amahl and the Night Visitors* one Christmas, which was an ambitious attempt unheard of before with classes so small and inexperienced.

Standing by the board in his double-breasted pin-striped suit, he taught his lessons with such clarity and enthusiasm that the material became almost self-evident. The sciences especially just came to life. As he taught, he made notes on the blackboard with headings and sub-headings so logically arranged that they were not only an aid to learning but were a lesson in note-taking as well as providing an excellent study guide for later.

His organizational skills were evident in many other areas in the community. He organized our high school bonspiel, which was also new to Cayley and we loved it.

He let us know he cared about our education—where we were going. He woke us up, engaged us in the learning, made it easy and made us laugh. He initiated a graduation dinner and dance for the graduates in 1949. This had never been done before in our little village. We graduated three girls and one boy and in giving each girl a first-ever corsage, he made it even more memorable.

When Mr. Lindstedt went from Cayley to the University of Alberta for his Bachelor of Arts degree, the students left behind knew they were missing someone remarkable in the field of teaching. He was a truly memorable teacher.

Words of Wisdom for a Future Premier

by Hon. Peter Lougheed

Winston Churchill
Central High School (Collegiate), Calgary

My most memorable teacher gave me a first-rate piece of advice at the very beginning of my political career. His words of wisdom influenced me throughout my entire public life.

The teacher's name—believe it or not—was Winston Churchill, and he was my Grade 12 physics teacher at Central High School in Calgary.

It was September 1946; I was 18 years old, thinking about running for student council president. I wanted to propose a $10.00 student activity fee as part of my campaign. The money would help fund student dances, field trips, club activities but I knew it would be a controversial plank in my campaign. I needed some sound, adult advice.

Why didn't I seek out my physical education teacher? Our life at that time was sports—football, basketball, twelve months a year of non-stop sports. Or even a teacher from one of my better academic subjects English, Latin, social studies?

But not my physics teacher. Physics, all the sciences, were my weakest subjects. That was obvious in my marks, and was confirmed on an aptitude test I took later that year. And why the gruff, almost frightening Mr. Churchill? He was a very imposing man—tall, heavy-set. He was a conservative dresser—always wore a suit with a vest in those days. And a very stern exterior manner that made all of us nervous.

Yet I sensed an underlying kindness and consideration to Mr. Churchill. Often I could see a twinkle in his eye. This guy wasn't as gruff as he pretended to be. And I knew he wouldn't beat around the bush. He would give me an honest answer.

So I made an appointment to see him at the end of the afternoon, told him about my interest in running for student council president. Then I asked his advice on the $10.00 student-levy idea.

"You know you might lose," he replied. Then he followed with words I have never forgotten: "People don't like paying levies or taxes of any kind."

Despite Mr. Churchill's cautionary words, I kept the $10.00 activity fee in my campaign platform. I made my presentation at a school assembly, won the election and became student council president for the school year 1946-47.

Something like 92 per cent of the student body willingly put up their $10.00. (By the way, that same aptitude test that scored me low on the sciences gave me top marks for persuasiveness!)

Still, Mr. Churchill's advice on the public's unwillingness to part with money stayed with me. I often thought of him and his words of wisdom during my years as Alberta premier. It wasn't just keep taxes low. More important, it was be honest with your constituents. Tell them what you intend to do with their money.

I still think of Mr. Churchill every workday morning, when I first sit down at my office desk in downtown Calgary. I have a pen-and-ink desk set given to me by Central High School students at the end of my year as student council leader. It is inscribed:

> *To Peter Lougheed*
> *"Thanks Pete"*
> *1947*

Mr. Churchill remains in my thoughts whenever I gaze out my office window and look towards the old Central High School building at 8 Street and 13 Avenue SW, now the home of Rundle College. I wonder how many other students Winston Churchill influenced over the years?

My High School Saviour— A No-Nonsense Nun

by Suzanne (Biron) Cuell

Sister Marie Luciana
St. Michael's High School, Pincher Creek

In the summer of 1946, when I was 15 years old, my parents sent me and four of my sisters to St. Joseph's Church in Cowley for confirmation instruction. We left our ranch early each morning, either riding double on horse-back or in a horse-drawn buggy. We travelled over the hills approximately nine miles.

On the first day as the twenty-five children filed into the quaint little church, we were told by Fr. Violini to stand up when the good Sister arrived. Suddenly we heard a clap, clap. We stood and stared in amazement as a petite nun in full black habit, strode up the aisle. She crossed herself, genuflected and wheeled around to face us. The long, black rosary beads that hung from her waist made a clicking sound. Her small oval face was completely banded in white starched cloth. She clutched her crucifix to her bosom. With her shining brown eyes and a little half smile, she said in a rather sophisticated manner, "I'm Sister Luciana from St. Michael's in Pincher Creek. I've come to teach you about the Holy Spirit, and the prayers you must know to be confirmed. All of you who wish to be confirmed, raise your hand." With that twenty-five hands shot up.

After three weeks, Sister Luciana made a lovely picnic for us, and presented each one with a Holy picture. As she was presenting the gift to me, she asked, "Suzanne will you be coming to St. Michael's in September?" Nodding, I replied, "Yes Sister, I will." She patted me on the cheek. I knew from that moment that we were forming a special bond.

My mother enrolled me in St. Michael's High School, as well as room and board in Kermaria Convent. The first year went by very well and I adjusted to the routine. But I was always glad to hurry across the grounds to school before class began, to have chats with Sister whenever possible, and do little chores for her such as watering plants, cleaning the boards and brushes.

The second year I had broken out of my shell—gained more friends—and in the early spring, two friends and I decided that we would shed the thick lyle stockings that were part of the dress-code. We were still in the navy uniforms and white blouses, so we did not think anyone would notice.

Well, someone snitched on us and reported us to Mother Superior at the convent. Promptly at 4:00 p.m., Mother Superior called us in and told us that we had broken the rules and must pack up our belongings and leave the convent. You can only imagine how shocked we were and in tears. My mother came to town and tried to find out why this was such a bad example for the other kids—she didn't get very far with the Mother Superior.

On Monday morning Sr. Luciana was waiting for us as we entered her class. She said, "Suzanne, Barbara and Dorothy I have to see you at once in my office." Sister Luciana looked so shaken up that we didn't know what to expect. Then she said, "Girls, I know that you were asked to leave the Convent, and Mother Superior has ordered me to expel you from St. Michael's as well. Now I've advised her that I'll do nothing of the kind. I even told her that she had no jurisdiction over my high school. In fact, if you girls go, I would go as well." There were a lot of tears; however this time tears of joy! I knew in my heart, this no-nonsense nun had become our saviour. Clearly the lesson I learned from this horrible experience, is that everyone deserves a second chance.

Sister Luciana remained a friend right up until she passed away. She loved my letters and especially my Christmas poems. She said in her last letter "Christmas would miss something without both." I will forever keep her in my prayers and in my heart.

We're Losing Our Teacher

by Mary Ann Kurucz

Freda (Sauter) Geuder
Victoria School, Calgary

We're losing our teacher again, I thought, our favourite teacher. We lost her once before and we were very sad and angry, too. We didn't understand then; we were only in Grade 2. She was the only teacher we had ever known. She was leaving us to get married. We couldn't understand why she could leave us for a husband.

Freda Sauter, circa 1950. *Courtesy: Mary Kurucz*

Each morning of Grade 1 and 2, I went to school eager to see my beautiful teacher, Miss Freda Sauter. I was anxious to see her and do well to please her. Her clothes were so elegant to a child whose clothes were purchased at rummage sales in church halls of wealthy congregations. While my clothes were always clean but old and ill-fitting, Miss Sauter wore memorable clothes like her black polka-dotted shirtwaist dress with the yoke and big box pleats in the skirt. Her rich brown Selby oxfords with Cuban heels had leather loops to lace up her shoes instead metal eyes like my scuffed old shoes. How I longed to have shoes like hers, to have a dress like hers, too. "Someday," I promised myself.

She treated us like children of worth, children she spoke to as "my boys and girls". She taught us to read. Dick and Jane, Tim and Spot and Puff became my daily friends. I longed to live in a white house with a picket fence and trees on Elm Street, not like our rooming house with all those steps I had to clean each Saturday.

75

As we learned to read with Miss Sauter, she encouraged us to go to the public library to borrow books to practice reading. So my sister and I walked the six blocks to the palace-like structure, the Memorial Park Library. I asked the librarian for books that Miss Sauter had read to the class. When I tried to read them myself, there were many words I could not read. I learned that I had much work to do before I could be as smart as Miss Sauter. Maybe I would need to read every book in the library.

She left us in 1950 with only memories of those two years in her class in the Bungalow, only memories until the mid-1980s when Victoria School held a reunion for all who had attended the school since its opening. There Miss Sauter, now Mrs. Freda Geuder, stood in the school yard in a dusty rose-coloured party frock with her hair swept up just as I remembered. She was looking for "my boys and girls". I was thrilled to see her, still elegant and beautifully made up. She remembered so many of us, even after thirty-five years. Or maybe she only said that to spare our feelings.

Afterward, I visited with her a number of times each year when she came to Calgary to visit her sisters. Each visit was followed by her expressive, neatly hand-written thank-you notes, symbols of a fading social custom she continued to the time of her death, a fading custom that she continued with grace. Even from her deathbed, Mrs. Geuder asked visitors to drop her thank-you notes in the mail.

Although I was no longer her student I continued to learn in our new relationship as adult friends. She set herself goals and accomplished them. In a time when few female teachers, especially primary grade teachers, rarely earned a degree, Miss Sauter earned a Bachelor of Education through years of summer school study.

She travelled widely and often—South America, the Caribbean, the Holy Land, and even Russia in her mid-80s. She memorialized each trip in scrapbooks filled with photos and delightful captions and descriptive journal passages that informed the reader with fact and humour, too. Each time we met, she asked where I had travelled since last we met. Each time, she inquired, as only teachers do, "Did you write that up? You must." In November 2004, we lost our teacher, our favourite teacher. I marvelled at how the woman who had taught us so much early in our lives continued to teach us right to the end, teaching by example to behave with grace and dignity in the most trying circumstance. We lost our teacher but hold dear her memory and all we learned from her.

Soaring With Eagles

by Jim Green

June (Crook) Phillips
Pincher Creek Public School, Pincher Creek

It was in Grade 3 with Miss Crook in Pincher Creek, the school year was 1949–50, that I experienced my blazing breakthrough. I remember it clearly as the year ballpoint pens came out but were quickly banned, since the early models managed to leak bilious blue blotches, like somebody stepping on huckleberries on the kitchen lino, about every two or three words.

Pincher Creek School. *Courtesy: Glenbow Archives*

This was in the old gothic two-storey, sand-coloured, stucco-sided Pincher Creek Public School that used to be on the east end of the field across from the United Church. There were several ball diamonds in the field where we played pum-pum-pullaway and kick-the-can at recess, and Fox and Geese in the snow in winter. It turned into a lake every spring which was the most fun of all. Spring was also marble season, and there was plenty of room for dozens of circles to be scratched out in the dirt with a stick. We boys played mumbley-peg with our pocket knives too, when no teachers were in sight.

There were graffiti-like blast marks on the outside walls around all the entrances of the school where kids had whapped the wood-backed felt blackboard erasers in futile attempts to get all the chalk out of them.

Miss Crook, now, she was a wonder. Besides urging us onward in improving our penmanship and giving us an early grasp of the difference between a noun and a verb, Miss Crook did something else for us. She read.

Every day after lunch, exactly at one o'clock, after the hand bell's pealing beckoned us from the school yard, after we'd swarmed inside in our raucous hordes and slung our jackets with the bags of marbles in the pockets on the long rows of brass coat hooks in the hall, kicked off our shoes and hustled to our desks and got settled in, the cacophony of chatter died down, dead quiet; Miss Crook would sit up on an empty desk at the front of the room facing us, sit on the top of the desk with her feet on the seat, and open the book—*Silver Chief, Dog of the North*.

Miss Crook read for the sheer pleasure, a novel and delightful notion. She loved the sounds of the words and she read with vivacious gusto, modulating her voice for the different characters, whispering through tense passages, pausing for effect. Miss Crook read from the heart, with a passion almost spiritual in its purity and intensity. That did it for me.

She took me by the hand and she showed me the way. You talk about being transported; my goodness. I was Peter Pan, flying out the window. I was lifted off, carried away and whisked to another world. I knew right then what I wanted. I wanted to learn how to read, and read well, so I could take wing whenever I wanted, to wherever I chose.

All the seemingly useless hours of exercises finally made sense to me. Learn how to make the letters so you could make the words. Learn how to make words so you can make sentences. Learn how to read sentences and paragraphs, stories, books, whatever, so you can take off. Anytime. Anywhere.

That was it. Miss Crook (she got married later and became Mrs. Phillips) was the teacher who opened up that other world. It was so simple. She just read to us. But she knew what she was doing. She opened the window for us so we could gaze out there and be smitten by the possibilities. She offered us opportunity. I was hooked.

Years later, after she'd retired from teaching school, June Phillips wrote a column for the Pincher Creek *Echo* for a time. She closed her January 9, 2001 column with a quote from Helen Hayes: "When books are opened you discover that you have wings."

Just so. With all my heart, I thank June Phillips for a fascinating and rewarding life soaring with eagles.

A Man for All Seasons

by Senator Dan Hays

Alfred Howard
Strathcona School, Calgary

Walking through the classrooms of my recollections, I see the faces of the many men and women who taught me and left an indelible impression by reinforcing my curiosity, encouraging my pursuit of knowledge and nurturing my spirit of adventure.

But the man who stands most prominently in this gallery of dedicated and talented educators is, without a doubt, Alfred Howard, who was headmaster of the Strathcona School from 1940 to 1967. I remember him as a man of broad vision and public spirit; whose teaching philosophy basically consisted of tapping the potential of all boys, and encouraging them to do their very best. To live, in

Alfred Howard. *Courtesy: Glenbow Archives*

short, according to the school's motto: *nil nisi optimum* (nothing but your best). His nurturing and encouraging of more average students, in particular, testified to his great democratic sensibility and profound belief in the virtually unlimited potential of all individuals.

It's in the late forties that I arrived at Strathcona School, which was located in an imposing stucco mansion by the Elbow River in southwest Calgary. It was a small school, something that greatly contributed to the family atmosphere pervading it, along with the presence of Mr. Howard's wife, Florence, who took care of the boarders, and that of their children, who also studied there. The first floor consisted of classrooms designed to accommodate the fifty or so students, while the boarders were lodged on the second floor. The basement, for its part, contained the lockers for day boys such as myself.

Alfred Howard became a teacher by accident, since a back injury had forced him to cut back on his activities as a farmer. But Mr. Howard took to education with great passion, imparting pluralist values and an egalitarian sensibility on generations of boys, providing them with a sense of duty, country and personal discipline.

At times, his respect for our institutions and traditions would even go somewhat beyond the pale. I remember that on the day following the death of King George VI—on February 7, 1952, he purposely led the singing of *God Save the King* one last time, out of loyalty to the late monarch—something deemed most inappropriate by the other teachers.

As an educator and mentor, he believed it was his purpose not only to provide knowledge, but to instil a sense of civic responsibility among his students. He knew that by encouraging them to think for themselves, as well as by absorbing and mastering the knowledge the school dispensed, students would be in a position to answer the call of citizenship, public participation and public service. And, as the record shows, many of them have done so. You might even say that he was a firm believer in Aristotle's maxim, that: "All those who have mused on the art of governing humanity are convinced that the fate of nations depends on the education of young people."

Alfred Howard was not only a wonderful teacher and mentor; he was a remarkable father-figure as well. I am forever indebted to him for helping shape my world view, and for giving me the learning tools needed to broaden my knowledge and find my way through the labyrinth of life.

Chapter 4
Teachers of the 1950s

Alberta was a province in transition during the decade of the 1950s. Economic growth was spurred by the Leduc oil boom, and benefited from the general prosperity that engulfed postwar North America. Economic diversity was apparent, as petroleum quickly rose to challenge agriculture and ranching as Alberta's dominant industry. Good times meant more money for highway construction, expanded social services, and new schools. Meanwhile, the population shift from rural and small town to larger city, first evident in the hard times of the inter-war years, continued apace during postwar prosperity.

Alberta's schools and school districts were also in transition. Rural consolidation schemes of the 1930s were now possible, thanks to better district roads and bright-yellow school buses. City boards expanded their high-school vocational offerings to serve extended teenage enrolment patterns and meet the employment needs of industry. This chapter reflects a changing province as it spotlights memorable teachers in such diverse settings as the few surviving one-room rural schools to the spanking new composite high schools of the cities.

While teaching in the 1950s brought relief from the grim years of depression and world war, it also confirmed that world events continued to impinge on student lives. Teachers of this decade taught through the political fallout of the Cold War and the scientific challenge of Sputnik. Please join in saluting a number of memorable teachers from these years: George Staal, Algie Brown, Frank Epp, Margaret Campbell, Phyllis Yaworski, Laurie Cottrell, Clarice Bush, Minnie Bosch, Margaret Graham, Elaine Harrison, Pearl Stubbe, Dorothy Hawley, and Alice Tyler.

Teacher and Principal

by Bonnie Laing

George Staal
Bowness Junior High School, Calgary

George Myron Staal. *Courtesy: Sharoyne Van de Gijr*

George Staal came to the hamlet of Bowness in 1935 to become the principal for the existing four classrooms which grew to twenty rooms, spread out in numerous locations. Until his death in 1954, George was the main official for the Bowness School District. He interviewed teachers, ordered all the supplies for the students and classrooms, met with dignitaries, and still taught a class. He didn't have any office staff to assist and "preparation time" didn't exist in those days.

I first met George Staal in 1950 when I was in Grade 7. I was fairly tall at the time and sat at the back of the room. Unfortunately I was also very short-sighted and had difficulty seeing the blackboard. Often I would lean over and ask a neighbouring student what some of the words were. This activity did not stand me in good stead with the Grade 8 teacher who taught some of our subjects. Often my talking was rewarded with a detention after hours.

Our school participated in a small rural organization for sports. As most of the schools involved were very small, it was required to have at least one girl on the school baseball team. For Grades 8 and 9 I was the sole girl on the team. Due to my previously mentioned "talkativeness", I frequently had to serve a detention on game day. I would suffer with anxiety worrying about what would be the consequences if I didn't show up for the game! Mr. Staal was a big man, well over six feet, and, when he walked down the hall in the converted barracks building which was our school, you could feel the vibrations from his footsteps. He would appear in the doorway and ask the teacher quietly if my detention was finished. She would nod "Yes," sometimes reluctantly, and he would say to me, "Come on Miss Paul you're going to be late for the game if you don't hurry." Then he would drive me to the game and often stayed to watch.

Although he was known as a firm disciplinarian, less known was that he encouraged his students and supported their endeavours in sports and citizenship. I was a "tomboy" and enjoyed all sports. He respected that interest and I was never discouraged from playing on the boys' teams or in the games at recess and noon hour. The opportunities for girls to participate in athletics in the early fifties were very limited, especially in a small community such as Bowness. His support for the participation of his students in sports was remarkable given the heavy workload he carried on behalf of the school district and his students.

His example made me realize that other interests, besides the academics, were equally important in developing good citizens, and that all students have special talents and interests which need to be recognized and encouraged. This was a lesson I tried to emulate during my twenty-seven years of teaching.

George Staal was a big man, not just in stature, but in the influence he had on many of his students. His expectations were high but fair and brought out the best in his students. After Grade 9, the Bowness students had to travel to Calgary for high school. Students could choose which of the five high schools they would attend. George Staal, working with the parents, put on a lovely graduation banquet and dance at our school, Bowness Junior High. Some students were going into the work force, and with the choice of different high schools we knew this was our last time together. The evening was a great success and a wonderful send off for the students. I know I will treasure the memories of that evening for the rest of my life. This short remembrance only touches on some of the things I know about this special teacher who made a difference in my life. His influence has lasted through the years and I know made me a much better teacher and person.

Still in Room 107

by Elizabeth Kirillo

Algie Brown
Victoria Composite High School, Edmonton

Sometimes, someone has an impact on a person's future and that person does-n't realize it until the future has become her past. This happened to me.

In 1951 and 1952, while attending Victoria Composite High School in Edmonton, Mr. A.R. Brown was my Grade 11 and 12 social studies teacher in room 107. He was an unassuming figure, probably in his late forties. Even though unremarkable looking, he received valid respect from the students because he gave equal regard to each student no matter what his or her gender, race or creed.

When he asked questions about current events, he involved not only the bright, but also the "weaker" students. Whether their response was a popular opinion or not, whether it had substance or was inflated to persuade—it didn't matter. He encouraged us all to have an opinion on global politics.

In 1952, with the Cold War in full swing, our class discussed the benefit of living in a capitalist or socialist society. Most students approved of democracy, a few espoused socialism, but one boy firmly believed that Marxist-Leninist Communism was the only way to achieve equality. This would incite a heated debate between the students. Since I had close relatives living in the Ukraine, I remember becoming quite agitated by this boy's comments and responded bluntly to them, feeling he was being very naive. But Mr. Brown patiently and calmly listened to both sides and sometimes played devil's advocate by using opposing arguments. He said our future depended on our insights and judg-ments. There is no doubt in my own mind that room 107 had the liveliest polit-ical discussions in the school.

After graduation, I had thought of going to the University of Alberta in Edmonton, hoping eventually to become a journalist. Mr. Brown knew of my plans. But in Grade 12, after I had met a young man who had finished his schooling, my plans changed. Love took me in a different direction. I told Mr. Brown that I was going to get married on the Labour Day weekend. Naturally, he was disappointed with my decision.

Through the next twelve years of being a stay-at-home mom, I couldn't shake off the nagging feeling that I had to complete some unfinished business. So in 1964, I announced to my husband and 10-year-old son that I was going to enrol in the four year Bachelor of Education program at the U of A. They had no objections. Those four years of trying to fulfill the roles of mother, wife, daughter to ailing parents and university student were difficult. Still, it was an exciting time in my life and all worth it. I was 38 years old when I graduated from university and my first teaching position took me back to my alma mater, Victoria Composite High School.

During my teacher's training I had often thought of my former social studies teacher, and how he had aspired to make young people knowledgeable about their place in the world. It was, therefore, a pleasant surprise when I walked into the teachers' lounge on my first morning and saw the same Mr. Brown sitting having coffee.

It was 1968 and he had changed very little since I last saw him in 1952. I asked if he remembered me, one of his favourite students. He laughed and said that he certainly did. I told him that I was a first-year teacher. He said that he was delighted that I continued with my education even if there was a delay. And yes, he was still in room 107—had been for seventeen years but would be retiring after the next term.

Now retired, I often think about how one man's teaching abilities had influenced my life in becoming a teacher. He taught us that integrity and honesty are our moral responsibilities. They are the building blocks for our beliefs and at the same time we had to understand that other societies did exist and it was the rights of individuals and groups to have dissenting opinions, but it was our duty to question and qualify and above all take nothing for granted.

Mr. Brown's journey as a teacher was to take his students to different places and to transform them from indifferent adolescents to caring adults with curiosity.

As a former teacher approaching my seventy-second year, I hope that I have travelled the distance without being diverted too many times onto a side road.

I thank Mr. A.R. Brown for being my invisible guide.

Guidelines to Live By
by Gordon Oborne

Frank Epp
Water Valley School, Water Valley

Water Valley School, 1952. Gordon Oborne—far left, front row. *Courtesy: Gordon Oborne*

In the fall of 1952, Frank Epp came to Alberta; he drove his new Chev Bel-Air over dusty gravel roads, about fifty miles northwest of Calgary, to the small hamlet of Water Valley. He moved into the little teacherage and prepared to teach the "big kids" (Grades 6, 7, 8 and 9) in the two-room rural school.

Because there were no school buses, and I lived on a ranch quite a distance west of Water Valley, each school year I boarded with a local family closer to the school. I was a student who had struggled through my early school years. But in Grade 8, Mr. Frank Wilfred Epp entered my life. He was to become my hero and my marks were to soar that year.

From the start of the day until we left at the end of the school day, Frank spent every minute with the class. He, of course, taught the main subjects—reading, writing and arithmetic—but most importantly he went the extra mile and taught us other things as well.

For shop, he bought a four by eight foot sheet of plywood and tying it to the top of his car, he brought it to school. There, he cut it into one-foot square pieces so that every student could create something by using a fret saw and some paint. I made my mother a chicken with two hooks to hang potholders on. As a joint project we built a crokinole board and then were all able to join in and play the game.

At recess he helped with sports joining right in and teaching us good sportsmanship.

But most importantly, he taught us good basic guidelines to live by. He told us to respect our elders, by listening to them, helping them with chores and opening doors for them. He told us that one day we would be seniors ourselves.

He also taught us about dating and told us that when you pick up your girl-friend, go to the door, treat her parents with respect, open car doors for her, walk on the outside to protect her and let her know that you are a gentleman.

Frank taught us that when you go out into the workforce be prepared to come home at night and look in the mirror and be able to say, "I did an honest day's work for an honest day's pay, without hurting anybody."

Frank Epp was, without a doubt, the one person, outside of my family, who has had the most influence on my life and I have tried to follow his guidelines throughout the years.

My Angel, My Mentor

by Roberta Volker

Margaret Campbell
Wood Lake School, Stettler

Roberta Volker. *Courtesy: Roberta Volker*

I attended one of the last one-room schools in Alberta—Wood Lake School. Mrs. J. Harold Campbell taught me Grade 1 to Grade 7, and then my family moved away. Grades 1 to 9 were taught in this one room; as well, a high school student did her correspondence courses at the back of the room. There were usually about twenty-five students enrolled each year.

Mrs. Campbell was the most wonderful, all encompassing individual who inspired us to do our very best every minute of every day by respecting us and bringing forth that feeling of self worth. She not only taught every subject to every grade, she had special-needs children to teach as well. I must mention one student who was hearing-impaired as well as mute. She provided for him a special program and used drama to bring him out. This young boy participated in all our activities and played an important part in all school plays and gatherings. He was truly included in our classroom and had no modern day aide to help him. Mrs. Campbell ingeniously had the rest of us help him, as well as each other.

Mrs. Campbell read the most interesting books in literature—they were the classics. We wrote wonderfully creative stories under her tutelage. Our art compositions were delightfully creative and have been kept over the years. She frequently had us create murals about our social topics and our pioneer unit, with its sculptures made from nature, left an ever lasting impression on our minds. Social studies took us outside building a pioneer log cabin, and pioneer transpiration had us build and float a raft. All were made with pioneer tools—axe and bucksaw. Science class took us out on plenty of nature finds to see wild orchids growing near the school as well as acorns being gathered by squirrels in preparation for winter. She had the ability to make every lesson come alive with her curiosity that she shared and passed on to us, her students. We all came away doing well in math because of her love of the subject and the fun projects she would create to make it real life experiences for us.

Margaret and Harold Campbell, Wood Lake School reunion, 1975. *Courtesy: Della Negal*

I have looked back over the years and marvelled at the social skills she incorporated in every day living. The energy she put into our Christmas concerts ensured that each child showed their talents and looked our best to the public. She inspired us to create artistic boxes for the box socials. The pie socials got moms baking with their children. At dances we learned to participate with our families at gatherings. She engaged the community to teach us square-dancing. We skated on a nearby slough until parents built us a boarded skating rink at the school grounds.

I remember the day I told her I was going to become a teacher. It was no surprise to her. Her comment was that she knew I would become a teacher because I had taught each incoming new Grade 1 class how to read since I was in Grade 3. I modeled myself after her teachings. I conducted my classroom in the same way she had. I have had a very successful and fulfilling career as a teacher and I have my angel, my mentor, Mrs. Campbell, to thank for that. I have loved every day in my classroom—just as she did. She earned the highest respect here on earth and I am sure her wings are now gold.

Her Smile Lit Up the Room

by Delsie Thachuk

Phyllis (Yaworski) Pentelechuk
Edwand School, Edwand (hamlet of Smoky Lake)

Edwand School was one of the many one-room schools in the School Division of Smoky Lake. It was located a half mile south of the hamlet of Edwand. It was a "prairie-typical" schoolhouse situated in a large yard surrounded by bush and trees. The yard also included a teacherage, a well, outhouses and the mandatory swings built by the parents of the community. The yard was large enough to allow some to play ball in the spring, chase butterflies, or pick dandelions.

It was the school my sisters and I attended in the early 50s when Miss Phyllis Yaworski came into my life. She had just completed her university training in Edmonton and this was her first placement. She was young, beautiful, enthusiastic, and her smile lit up the room.

I had just passed into Grade 7 and was curious and somewhat afraid of this newcomer. Her demeanour and gentleness soon dispelled my fears and she won me over. It became apparent to all of us that Miss Yaworski meant business! She expected our best efforts in our studies and nothing else would do. We soon learned to make sure our homework was done and our projects finished on time.

It was in the area of the arts that Miss Yaworski excelled and it wasn't long before we were all involved. Miss Yaworski did not believe in the word "can't". To supplement our physical education program, she managed to convince the Smoky Lake High School gym teacher to lend us their gymnastics equipment. They even delivered it! She then introduced the world of gymnastics to all of us at Edwand School. We were soon performing triple somersaults, backward bends, splits and flying over the box-horse. She encouraged us to work in teams and put together creative routines using the equipment. There we were performing, encouraging and spotting each other.

Then she encouraged (actually directed) us to take our show on the road. So we did! We put on performances around the Edwand area—usually before the country dances started.

Miss Yaworski was not satisfied with performing the same routines day after day—she encouraged us to develop new themes and incorporate new movements. We did not have any spare time—we were busy creating!

She borrowed a record player and taught us tap-dancing, square-dancing and folk-dancing. My classmates and I took our dancing skills seriously and before long were entering a variety of community talent shows—often humming or singing our own accompaniment. To this day, friends around Smoky Lake remind me of my dancing "expertise"! And until the last year of my teaching career, I taught the same dances I learned from Miss Yaworski.

Friday afternoons were often spent perfecting or performing the "arts". We practiced our gymnastics or dance routines and choral arrangements. The older students assisted the younger ones and everyone participated. Friday afternoons were a joy, because Miss Yaworski taught us the basics and then gave us the opportunity to "fly" in a safe environment.

When I entered Grade 9, Miss Yaworski moved to teach home economics at H.A. Kostash School in Smoky Lake. She also became Mrs. Pentelechuk and she and her husband, Nick, made their home in the Town of Smoky Lake.

Mrs. Pentelechuk continued to be part of my life during my high school years. She listened, counselled and listened some more. She did not impose her ideas; just guided me and let me make my own decisions. I'll always remember seeing her stand beside my parents at my graduation. She was so proud of me.

I attended the University of Alberta, became a teacher and met my husband. Mrs. Pentelechuk baked our wedding cake and wished us well.

She always implied that my (our) future extended beyond the school environment or the community. She talked about the world and how fortunate we were to have the opportunity to get an education and to travel. She said it was our responsibility to contribute to society in a meaningful way.

Mrs. Pentelechuk succumbed to breast cancer in 1982, but her spirit lives on in the student she taught at Edwand School. She believed in me and she instilled in me the confidence I needed to believe in myself. Her principles often guided me in the teaching of my own students. I wish my sons could have met her, because so often her principles guide their lives too.

Mister "C"

by Kathleen Smith

Laurie Cottrell
Airdrie High School, Airdrie

Being a country girl and a rancher's daughter made it necessary to ride on horseback to a rural, one-roomed school for my education from Grades 1 through 9. A more intimidating time came when I was obliged to attend high school in Airdrie, where I was completely unfamiliar with the system. Grade 9 had been spent with eight other students, one in each of the nine grades. Now there were twenty-two students in my new surroundings in the early 1950s where Mr. Laurie Cottrell taught high school and was the principal of the four-roomed structure. I was very unsure of myself in these new premises, but the stately gentleman that I still fondly keep in touch with, gave me confidence to overcome my insecurities. He instilled in me a lasting knowledge of who and what I wanted to become. Laurie taught all subjects to our varied high school class. If we tried hard and did well, he praised us, but if we didn't, he found a way to deal with our inadequacies. His sense of humour was ever present, but when we tested his tolerance, we knew we would pay for our mischief.

Physical education was left largely to the students, as there were no organized teams for sports as there are now. We walked the sidewalks or made up our own games. During the winter months, we were sometimes allowed to go skating on the frozen creek that ran beside the town's grain elevators, now non-existent in many prairie towns. One day, not being an accomplished skater, I caught my blade on a broken beer bottle frozen in the ice and fell on it. One eyebrow was sliced neatly open, and blood flowed freely down my face. Laurie Cottrell cleaned me up and took me in his little car to our family doctor in Calgary where several stitches were applied.

When I was in Grade 11, our English class was shown a picture of a deteriorating, deserted house on the desolate prairies. Mr. Cottrell asked us to write a story about our perception of why the house had become an empty skeleton.

My math and chemistry skills were minimal, probably because my previous one-roomed schoolhouse had taught less efficiently with nine grades to educate by one over-worked teacher. But English was always my easiest subject, so without hesitation, my story entitled "Deserted" took the form of a poem. It was then that Laurie asked what I wanted to do when I was finished high school. In 1952 there were few choices for a girl of 16 to choose from, and I was considering nursing at the time. He told me to follow my heart, but he thought journalism would be a better choice for me than nursing.

I didn't become a nurse, and I didn't take journalism either, but I did follow my heart. I married at 18 and had two children, and now I have six grandchildren. I kept the poem that I wrote in Grade 11 at Airdrie High School, and now on Alberta's 100th birthday, I am still in touch with Laurie Cottrell who has been retired for many years and lives in Victoria, British Columbia. Five years ago I started writing again, and occasionally share my stories with him. He continues to encourage me to write more, and says the natural ability is still with me.

Laurie Cottrell is an exceptional man, a most competent teacher and principal, and an exemplary human being. He instilled confidence in me at an early age, and his teachings will always be a fondly remembered part of me.

Mrs. Bush Says . . .

by Lynne (McConnell) Miedreich

Clarice Bush
Nampa Public School, Nampa (southeast of Peace River)

Marco Polo, warmly dressed against the minus twenty degree weather, walking stick clutched in heavily-mittened hand, stands gazing with curious anticipation across the vast expanse of snowdrifts stretching eastward. The late afternoon sun touches the crusted surface ahead with regal golds and purples. He peers into the beyond, sees these last majestic miles before him into the court of the great Kublai Khan, into the land his father has told him about—the land of fine silks, spicy ginger, vast cities and brisk trade. He is eager to push on, but his companion says firmly, "We must eat." They hunker down in a snow bank out of the wind and quietly munch on peanut butter sandwiches and oatmeal cookies. The year is 1955. . .

I no longer remember if my best friend, Sheila, and I actually discussed who would be Marco Polo and who would be his father. What I do remember vividly is that I *was* Marco Polo on that thrilling after-school trip across the Gobi Desert (alias Eric Roger's neighbouring snow-covered summer fallow), lost in a world of medieval exploration, my heart pumping in expectation, my mind swirling with images of other places and other times—all conjured up in my Grade 5 class by Mrs. Bush, a teacher I shall be eternally grateful for.

A 20-year-old Camrose Normal School graduate, Mrs. Bush had come to our small northern community to teach in 1927, married a local homesteader within the year, then settled down to raise a family. During the war years she was enticed back to teaching at Nampa Public School where I had the good fortune to fall into her hands at the start of my Grade 3 year in 1953. She was to be my teacher and my idol for the next three years. Mrs. Bush's loudly enthusiastic hands-on teaching style created within me a fierce loyalty to her and my mantra at home became, "Mrs. Bush says. . ."

The goings on in our classroom were met with much rolling of eyes, and I suspect, some envy by other students at Nampa Public School, and apparently the subject of more than one acerbic comment by more traditional staff. My older sister, whose teacher didn't think much of the clatter coming from down the short hall, let me know that we were a source of annoyance. I was incensed. I loved that room and I loved Mrs. Bush, and I defended her vehemently. It wasn't until years later, when my sister wrote a poem gently poking fun at my idol worship, that I began to realize how much of an influence Mrs. Bush really did have on me.

Before educational catch-phrases like *subject integration, discovery learning, peer teaching,* or *group work* were in vogue, Mrs. Bush had set up a store at the back of our classroom, complete with empty tins, boxes and cartons from which we learned geography, economics, trade, and math skills. She had us creating huge and colourful timelines on long rolls of brown paper from my Uncle Mill's general store. On these we charted and illustrated the progression of historical events, then proudly waited for Mrs. Bush to wrap the upper wall of our classroom with them. We formed into noisy but productive groups to work on reports, role-played historical events, partnered up to learn our times tables. I listened in awe to her life stories and to her embellishment of our curriculum from her own readings, as well as her prognostications about the future.

I can close my eyes still and see her full-skirted square frame, her full red lip-sticked mouth, hear her cigarette-husky voice as she reads to us from *The Water Babies* or *Huckleberry Finn*. A truly intuitive teacher, Mrs. Bush left me with a love of learning and some sound practical advice which has served me well: when my eyes are tired, I should put down my pencil and look out at the healing green of the trees; everybody (including kids) deserves a fair shake; little toes may disappear if our feet don't do more walking; there is no such thing as *can't!* I am indebted to her for the remarkable gifts that she gave me.

She Accepted Me Where I Was At

by Jeanne (Verbeek) Lutgen

Minnie (Bosch) Cournoyer
Cunningham School, Morinville

It was my first day to go to school. I was going for two long weeks before the summer holidays. It was to introduce us to the whole process, preparing us for Grade 1 after the holidays. Only five years old, I had never been away from my parents for long, as both mom and dad were stay-at-home parents—I was to go away from this safe haven! I was scared!

I was happy to have my big brother and sister with me to go down our lane to the bus; the bus was so noisy and the kids were so big. The bus driver was even bigger and scarier. When we got to school, my sister showed me where my class was located, however she had to go to her class, so left me to go in alone. I stepped up to the open door and standing there was this little lady in high heels—she was almost my size—and she had a big smile! She put her arm around me and said that she was my teacher, Miss Minnie Bosch, and asked me my name. She said she knew who I was and that she was waiting for me. She walked me to a desk and patted me on the head as I sat down. I felt a bit better; she seemed so friendly and caring.

That was my first introduction to my favourite teacher. Our relationship grew to one that is still alive to date. She helped me with my dilemma of writing with my left hand instead of my right. She assured my father, at a parent-teacher interview that, "Jeanne is so comfortable writing with her left hand so let's leave her do so" and that "it was perfectly acceptable." She helped me by accepting me where I was at and did not trivialize the personal struggles that I or any of her students were having. She became my role model, someone I wanted to be like when I grew up.

As my older brother and many of her other students still in this community say, she was loving, caring, motherly, and not intimidating, yet kept the class disciplined. If anyone was making noise as she was talking or reading one of her many wonderful storybooks (which she kept in her closet) after dinner she would look at that person, tap her heel on the floor or say "shhh!" to them. Her closet also held a little present for the birthday boy or girl. She did not forget those having birthdays during the holidays.

Many remember the music. We all had wonderful singing voices according to her as she laughed at some off-key voices. She saw the potential and the efforts. She was so talented at playing the piano that she was the main wheel of each year's exciting Christmas Concert, playing for all the grades. Her piano accompanied all musicals, or plays, wherever music was needed even with the games we played for fun or gym or exercise time. She was a good sport too, as many children chose her as the one tagged "You're It!" while being the fox in the "Fox and the Goose".

One student said she always started the day cheerfully, after prayers, with the song: *Good Morning to you! Good morning to you! We're all in our places with sun shiny faces. Oh this is the way to start a new day.*

Another student said, "When your day was going bad or you got hurt she would say, 'Oh poor dear'!" Another said how he remembered the parties we had—every student got to bring some home-made treat and share it with the class.

My one brother remembers that she always seemed to have a soft spot in her heart for all her students and when meeting them in the hallways or out in public she would always make a fuss over seeing you and was always interested in your progress through your schooling and life. He said, when older and going to the high school across town, he and other students would occasionally go back to Cunningham School to see her. You would not have a student do that if a teacher had not made a difference in their lives.

My sister remembered the school excursions to go see the local mink farm at the edge of town operated by Mr. Paul Cournoyer. She remembers that he would patiently answer all the questions that twenty-five plus students could ask. Miss Bosch would say how nice that man was. She later married him.

She was the best teacher for Grade 1 and 2 students, helping shy or scared little children. She was a positive influence on each child's life, giving us all a good start on this our education journey. She was, and is, an example of what it means to be a good teacher. Thank you, Miss Bosch!

The Smartest Person in the World

by Maureen A. McLeod

Margaret Graham
Cold Lake School, Cold Lake

At twelve I was on the edge of adolescence, a somewhat precocious and very responsible female child, the eldest for seven (soon to be eight) siblings born into a strict, but loving, Roman Catholic family whose parents were first-generation off the prairie homestead. We lived at the end of the highway in Cold Lake, a small town clinging to the shores of its namesake lake where my father was both principal of the only school and mayor.

It was September 1957. The western world was about to be shocked out of its educational complacency by a small bundle of electronics named Sputnik, and I was about to meet my most memorable teacher. She was a lovely and lively white-haired Protestant lady, small in stature but large of heart, whose official credentials were minimal but whose actual ability was phenomenal.

As ours was the only Grade 8 class, Mrs. Graham taught us everything we were to learn that year. She was tough when she needed to be; empathetic when we needed her to be; and the smartest person in the world—or so I thought at the time.

She would rejoice with us when our exam results were good and admonish us just enough when they weren't. She could talk knowledgeably about professional wrestling with one of the boys who was a great fan of the sport, or she could bring her yardstick cracking down of the desk of that same boy should his attention to the lesson wander.

Every day she filled the blackboards that marched around three of our classroom's four walls with her elegant spidery longhand, while we attempted valiantly to keep up with her pace. She seemed to have an endless capacity for distilling history and science into well-organized notes. I still remember the exciting Tudor kings and queens and the ill-fated Stuarts who followed them; Eli Whitney and the cotton gin; Leeuwenhoek and his microscope; James Watt and the steam engine. I still see the seemingly endless grammar rules that came to reign over our young lives. I can still hear her drumming algebra with its unknowns and its complicated equations into my friend's head. "X is only your name" was her oft-repeated litany.

Mrs. Graham instilled in me a love of the marvellous true stories in British history and, indeed, in all of history—a love I try very hard to impart to my own Grade 5 students today. She showed me the human side of science and, although science is not my forte, I still enjoy the fascination behind the facts and sincerely hope I have helped my students to do so too. She helped me unravel the mysteries of math and, although numbers and I have never been the best of friends, I continue to carry with me an innate sense of the logic of math. As for English, what can I say about a teacher who recognized and helped to nurture the budding writer hidden within my clumsy adolescent attempts to capture the world in words?

When it comes to the non-academic side of school, I can still picture all of us out on the school ground playing scrub ball on a sunny afternoon in late spring. While I excelled in the classroom, the playing field seemed to belong to everyone else. Even so, my classmates knew that Mrs. Graham would brook no criticism of those of us who showed much more enthusiasm than talent for the game. Thus, I was always encouraged to "take your walk" rather than reviled for my clumsy inability to connect bat to ball. Perhaps it is due in part to her that I still love the game—as a spectator.

Long after I left the school and the town, I continued to correspond with this amazing but unassuming teacher who soon took on the role of my unofficial mentor and life-long friend. Sadly she died many years ago after what I hope was a relaxing retirement in the much warmer climate of southern British Columbia.

Thank you, dear lady.

A Young Breath of Fresh Air

by Patricia (Davison) Triska, Donah (Forry Hunt) Reid,
Florence (Kenzie) Landy and Ron Campbell

Elaine Harrison
Hamilton Junior High School, Lethbridge

Room 30 Angels' 40th reunion. Front row left to right: ELAINE HARRISON, Kathy Evans, Dale Rider, DONAH REID. 2nd row left to right: FLORENCE LANDY, Andrea Craig, RON CAMPBELL, PATRICIA TRISKA, Gailene Shaw, Judy Amundson. *Courtesy: Patricia Triska*

Hamilton Junior High in Lethbridge was a lot different in 1957–1958. Our school, a two-story brick, was old even then—built in 1928 if our memory is correct. It looked like it could, and possibly had, withstood the forces of nature over time. We "lived" on the second floor in a centre compound with only a skylight for a window. Our Grade 7 desks were joined by rails to the floor with flip-top wooden lids that bore the marks of our predecessors. Those desks were a great way not to be seen by the simple raising of the lid, and they also doubled as shields in times of war. A real slate blackboard was at the front, along with the standard-of-the-day teacher's desk. We don't recall it being an overly tasteful place.

Our homeroom teacher, Elaine Harrison, was a different story. She was a young breath of fresh air and it was her first year teaching. She was on the "artsy" side of things and she taught us English. She was kind and caring, and thought we were special from day one.

The school year of 1957–58 disappeared into high school, followed by more school, marriages, jobs, reunions, families, "baby" angels for the kids, and finally grandchildren. Our teacher kept track of everything; a newsletter every January to keep everyone up on things, and a phone call if you forgot to do your part in supplying the necessary information. It has now been forty-eight years and each year her newsletter has become more special to each of us.

Christmas 1957 we started what would be a long tradition by getting together and buying a gift and a card for Mrs. Harrison, which we signed "Your Room 30 Angels" and angels we were to Mrs. Harrison and angels we still are.

We are all approaching sixty now, and after all this time, Grade 7 doesn't seem such a great distance away as the bonds with Mrs. Harrison and each other continue. On behalf of "Your Angels", we would like to say, "Thanks, Mrs. Harrison, you're the best!"

Reach for the Sky

by Peter Kent

Pearl Stubbe
Viscount Bennett School, Calgary

A lot of teachers went an extra mile—and many more—for me over the course of my erratic dozen years in the Alberta public school system. I was not a good student. I did not properly engage in the academic process. I squandered opportunities made available by a number of caring educators. My parents were comforted by the fact that there were four other children with a more appropriate affinity for the learning process.

That said—one teacher stands out among the many professionals who laboured long and hard to push louts like me through senior matriculation. Miss Stubbe was my homeroom teacher in Grade 8 at Calgary's Viscount Bennett Junior High. She was also my English teacher. A woman of diminutive stature—her name pronounced "Stubby"—she endured, with good humour, the "size" jokes of successive waves of oafish 13-year-old boys.

I remember clearly the day Miss Stubbe dispatched me from the familiar confines of classroom 8-22 to the unfamiliar precincts of the Viscount Bennett library, determined to wring a passable book report from one of her most uninspired students. I was told to go to the library, to scan the shelves, and to return only when I had a book—of at least 200 pages, she insisted—that "interested" me. An unlikely goal, I thought, meandering through the aisles farthest away from the authority figures behind the library counter. The shelves of well-handled volumes—most re-bound in the dreary blues, greens and purples favoured by school boards in the early fifties—seemed to hold nothing of great interest. But then, a new addition to the shelves, still wearing its original cover, caught my eye.

Reach for the Sky, the black block letters of the title proclaimed, over an artist's depiction of a banking Spitfire. The subtitle, in bright yellow, explained that this was "The Story of Douglas Bader—Hero of the Battle of Britain". On the first page, promotional paragraphs provided a hint of the stirring contents of Paul Brickhill's biography of the Second World War ace.

I was hooked. I devoured the book, marvelling at Bader's lonely childhood, the pre-war accident that claimed both of his legs, his uphill battle to get back into the Royal Air Force, his amazing accomplishments in the Battle of Britain, the dozens of enemy aircraft he shot down, the ultimate downing of Bader himself . . . and his unlikely escape from the notorious German prisoner-of-war facility, Colditz Castle.

My parents were pleasantly surprised by my account of the experience . . . although I'm sure they would have preferred a Waugh or Fitzgerald or Hemingway for my reading breakthrough. Miss Stubbe was satisfied, if not with my book report, with the simple fact that she'd won another young dolt to the world of books.

A few years later—by then a Sea Cadet, intent on a flying future with the Royal Canadian Navy—I had the honour of actually meeting Douglas Bader— Sir Douglas Bader by then. The conversation was all too brief. I remember blurting out how much his story had meant to me, while trying, without success, to determine whether he was still using the much-repaired pair of prosthetic legs that carried him through so many heroic adventures during the war years.

Decades later, Bader was interviewed by a young South African journalist. She was enchanted by the then 70-year-old's engaging "bulldog ferocity", his description of "fright—not terror" when there were "bullets in the cockpit", and by his humility.

Bader revealed to her that he only viewed the film *Reach for the Sky* eleven years after its release. "Saw it at home on a Battle of Britain Sunday. On television. Could've gone to the premiere, but didn't want to steal Kenneth More's thunder. It was his night, y'know. Thoroughly enjoyed it." That quote, on a yellowed clipping of the interview, was placed before me when I sat down at the kitchen table with the Toronto Public Library's well-handled Fontana paperback edition of *Reach for the Sky* to compose this piece.

Re-reading the article by the young journalist—now my wife—made for a serendipitous moment. Cilla's column, from a 1980 edition of the Johannesburg Star, also provides a much better read than my original, long-lost book report.

I wish Miss Stubbe had been around to read it.

She Gave Us Her "Joie de Vivre"

by Leslie (MacDowell) Duchak

Dorothy Hawley
Viscount Bennett School, Calgary

Dorothy Hawley was a legend before she came to Calgary's brand-new Viscount Bennett High School in the late fifties. Miss Hawley had taught French at Western Canada High School and her reputation preceded her. While we knew we were blessed to have a teacher who actually spoke French in Anglophone Calgary, she was a formidable personality.

Dorothy Hawley had studied at the Sorbonne, in Paris, and did not allow English in her classes. While many of us had taken French as an option in junior high, it would be generous to say that at that time, for the most part, our "oral French" was somewhat fractured.

Miss Hawley was a passionate individual, and among her passions were the French language, teaching, learning and opera. Her methods forced students to think in French. New material was reviewed the next day with a quiz, and four or five lucky students got to take their quiz at the blackboard and endure humiliation if they had not studied. Miss Hawley knew that when material was reviewed and recalled, there was more likelihood that it would be retained.

She used any device possible to explain grammar, vocabulary, history, culture. Indeed we wondered if she wouldn't stand on her head if she thought she could make it easier for us to understand!

Often we would learn the rules of French grammar by singing them to catchy tunes or opera arias. This may seem odd today, but we did it because it worked, and even though we did so sheepishly, it was difficult to ignore Miss Hawley's enthusiasm. It was said that at a university French exam you could always find Miss Hawley's former students, as they would be quietly singing grammatical songs to themselves. At our twenty-fifth reunion, it was stunning how we could still sing the rules and idioms thanks to her ingenious adaptations.

104

Miss Hawley set high standards, and most of us didn't want to disappoint her. Although somewhat eccentric, she showed, by her example, that there were clever ways to learn, and that learning was a matter of determination and work and that we could all succeed. Her own personal philosophy was that the mind was a powerful instrument which could help one overcome seemingly insurmountable obstacles.

Dorothy Hawley's legacy, as with most teachers, is impossible to measure. She belonged to an unsung group of teachers in Calgary who promoted the French language in an exclusively Anglophone environment and encouraged the movement towards bilingual education. I became a French teacher as did several of her students, and I am proud to say I used some of her pedagogical techniques.

Miss Hawley passed away in 2001 at the age of 93, and I was not surprised to see many of her former students at the memorial service. Most of us remember only a few of our teachers. It is safe to say that any student who had Miss Hawley would never forget her. She had a bigger-than-life persona and, although strict, she had an engaging smile and melodic laugh. Her gifts to her students were the precious gifts of all unforgettable teachers. Dorothy Hawley, by her example, gave us her *joie de vivre*, her joy of learning, her belief that with effort we could all succeed, and that anything is possible.

Chief Colour Co-ordinator

by Barbara (Reece) Leary

Alice Tyler
Queen Elizabeth Junior High School, Calgary

Alice Tyler receiving 1995 Governor General's
Award from Rt. Hon. Roméo LeBlanc.
Courtesy: Barb Leary

Alice Tyler—what can I say? In teacherdom, she was an icon. In an era when female teachers dressed conservatively in beige and grey suits, Alice was flamboyantly attired in hot pink and orange—and her signature jewellery. She was, after all, the art teacher and she played the role to the hilt!

Flashback to the summer of '57. All the kids in Grade 7 were telling we Grade 6 graduates what a witchy gypsy she was—she of the jet-black hair and dangly hoopy earrings that were actually bracelets . . . no kidding! So you can imagine the sheer fright that besotted our wee brains over that expectant summer.

On the first day of Grade 7 at Queen Elizabeth Junior High, Alice swept dramatically into the art room prompting one poor girl to pee her pants! We soon learned that a squeaked chair was reason enough to be sent to the principal's office—and Lord forbid you should squeak the chalk on the board!

She also had an aversion to using the colours orange and blue together, and so, when the Alberta Government chose that combination for licence plates, she blithely painted over hers, claiming that they "didn't match" the colour of her car. Fines and court cases ensued, but Alice, ever the crusader, emerged from the experience unscathed.

Many times she piled three or four of us into her Pontiac convertible for a trip to the local Dairy Queen (her treat). As young university students, Alice would regularly include us in her entertainment schedule. At one of her parties, a French maid took coats at the door while several tuxedo-clad waiters served us champagne and hors d'oeuvres . . . we had arrived!

Alice painted portraits of the *Famous Five*—Nellie McClung, Emily Murphy, Irene Parlby, Louise McKinney and Henrietta Muir Edwards, which now hang prominently in the Alberta Legislature and the Edmonton Law Courts building.

In 1990, when the class of '60 held its thirtieth reunion, the committee produced a mini yearbook, *Blast from the Past* in which they talked about our accomplishments and lives. One category was "Historical Data". Under Alice's they wrote "Hysterical Data"! They also noted she had been "Chief colour co-coordinator for Alberta Department of Highways, licence plate colours sub-committee."

Alice was a great inspiration to me—recognizing my artistic talents and encouraging me to attend the interior design faculty at the University of Manitoba. Years later when I was the mother of a very artistic son, we would see Alice at the local grocery store, resplendent in white fur from head to toe—a vision of Russian princessness! I would say to my Paul, "There's Miss Tyler"—and I could see she inspired an air of awe in my little boy too.

Despite her eccentricities, Alice was a talented and committed teacher who went on to receive the Governor General's award for her tireless work on the Persons' case. I was privileged to have been invited by Alice to attend the Person's Day ceremony when the *Famous Five* sculpture was unveiled in 1999, where I met Governor General, Adrienne Clarkson.

In retrospect, perhaps we artistic students were the children she never had. Alice and I kept in close touch until her death in 2001. I will forever be indebted to Miss Alice Tyler—she surely was my most memorable teacher.

Chapter 5
Teachers of the 1960s

For Alberta educators and their colleagues across the country, the 1960s were years of challenge, excitement, confusion and exhaustion. By that time, postwar "baby boom" children were moving into the senior grades, and school boards across Alberta scrambled to provide additional classrooms and more diversified high-school programs. In terms of physical growth, the expansion of the province's urban school systems far surpassed the early twentieth-century years of record development.

Even more significant were the radical social changes that began to sweep over Alberta—and North American—schools during the latter part of the decade. Adèle Kent, a student at Calgary's A.E. Cross Junior High School in the early 1960s, opens this chapter by recalling that she was "a product of the golden age of public education . . . just before the time when teachers and students started to concern themselves with the problems of drugs and then violence in the schools."

Social change influenced curriculum innovation and radical teaching approaches. The 1960s were a decade like no previous one in educational history, as teachers were confronted with new reasons for learning, new programs, new concepts to learn, and new ways of learning. Round tables began replacing straight rows of desks in elementary classrooms, while science fairs and 1967 Centennial projects captured the imagination of older students.

Through these years of change, Alberta's teachers proved up to the challenge of a new generation of young people. In this chapter's final selection, Dave Jorgensen, a student at Edmonton's Hardisty Junior High School, retains lifelong memories of his teacher's innovative haiku lessons at the end of the decade.

Teamwork

by Adèle Kent

Valerie Seaton, Lorraine (Smallwood) Patrick and Don Williams
A.E. Cross Junior High School, Calgary

I am a product of the golden age of public education in Calgary. It was just before the time when teachers and students started to concern themselves with the problems of drugs and then violence in the school. As a result, choosing my most memorable teacher was a difficult task. I was stumped not because I did not have any good memories of my teachers, but because I had a long list of memorable teachers.

From that long list, I have chosen three. Because they worked together and it was part of that teamwork that was so effective, I think that my description of them qualifies. The three teachers are Miss Seaton, Mrs. Patrick (Smallwood) and Mr. Williams, all physical education teachers at A.E. Cross Junior High School when I was there.

They were young, energetic teachers who not only taught the usual physical education classes, but organized a number of sports and social activities which we were all encouraged to participate in. We learned how to square dance, we had hootenannies and the gym was always full of team sports—volleyball, floor hockey and basketball. Because of the number of games being played in any one day, some of us were given the chance to learn how to be referees. I loved that. Maybe that is why I enjoy my current job so much!

But, in addition to learning new dances and winning strategies in basketball, we were taught more subtle, more powerful lessons. We were taught to have the confidence to try new things, to give everyone a turn, to work as a team and excel individually, and to have fun. Personally, it also dulled my somewhat overdeveloped competitive streak, at least for a while. Most of all, they taught us how important it was to be part of a community. Different kids were given different jobs—ringing the bell in the morning, selling donuts at the Friday afternoon dances, and so on. But, it all fit together. From the time that we arrived at school each morning until the last class (or more importantly, the last game) the school was a comfortable, yet invigorating place to be.

For me, there were two valuable results. First, I liked school. I remember lots of good days and no bad ones (although I am sure there were a couple). Second, I made good friends while I was at A.E. Cross, friends that I count among my best friends today, over 40 years later. I attribute a good part of this to the work of Miss Seaton, Mrs. Patrick and Mr. Williams.

A Dedicated Teacher of the Deaf

by Charmaine Letourneau

Elizabeth Palate
Alberta School for the Deaf, Edmonton

The obituary in the *Edmonton Journal* referred to Miss Elizabeth Palate as "a dedicated teacher at the Alberta School for the Deaf for almost 30 years. She touched the lives of all who knew her, especially the students and young people who shared her lively interest in the world around her." Truer words than these were never spoken.

Miss Palate was a *legend*. Stories about her have been passed down from graduating class to graduating class. Even young people today, who have never met her, know about her through stories told affectionately by former students and colleagues. Miss Palate was eccentric in many ways, but this made her the most interesting of characters.

Miss Palate was a very intelligent woman. We were often in awe of her knowledge of almost everything. We called her a walking encyclopaedia. We loved to test her vocabulary knowledge. We would pour over the dictionary trying to find the longest and weirdest words to challenge her. Miss Palate always knew the answers no matter how hard we tried to stymie her. Eventually we found out she cheated—she knew Latin, and so could figure out the meaning of almost any word.

Miss Palate was a very strict teacher. She would make us learn non-stop. She kept pushing books onto us and giving us a mile-high pile of homework every night. We had no choice but to read them and to do our homework to keep her off our backs. Miss Palate would stay late at the school and go into the dorm to see how we were doing with our homework. When she saw that we had finished her homework, she would give us more. All of our other subjects, except English, suffered. Even our love lives suffered.

Miss Palate loved books . . . of any kind. She had hundreds and hundreds of novels in her classroom. Every time we talked with Miss Palate about something, the first thing that came to her mind would be a book about something similar to what we'd just discussed. With all the novels in her classroom, Miss Palate knew exactly where each of them was and she would go directly to that spot to fetch us the books to read for homework. When we returned the books, Miss Palate would quiz us so you can bet that we READ! Miss Palate and I corresponded during the summer. I wrote to her about being bored at home way up north in a small hamlet and told her that I had read all the books in the library which had about fifty books. Know what Miss Palate did? She packed a large box of books and drove all the way to Smith, Alberta from Edmonton to deliver them to me—that was a three-hour trip one way.

Miss Palate enjoyed attending plays. She wanted her students to experience and enjoy the plays as she did. She collected newspapers and pop cans to pay for our tickets to different plays or movies. To make room in her car for the papers and pop cans, Miss Palate removed the back seat and the passenger seat leaving only the driver's seat. Getting money for us to see the plays was more important to Miss Palate than the look of her car. She also used her car to take us places. We would manage to squeeze into her car atop the newspapers and pop cans.

Miss Palate always had faith in us, deaf or not. She would relentlessly push us to learn more and more till we felt like screaming ENOUGH, ENOUGH. But now, we are very grateful for all she taught us. Miss Palate was my mentor, my "bestest" teacher. She was always there for me from my school days to college days to my teaching days. She helped to make me what I am today—a successful deaf person. Opening the world of knowledge for me through the joy of reading was her greatest gift. There can't be a better teacher than that one eccentric, strict, but loveable and dedicated teacher anywhere! She was the one and only, Miss Palate.

She Worked a Kind of Teaching Magic

by Suzanne North

Phyllis Weston
Crescent Heights High School, Calgary

Crescent Heights High School, Calgary.
Courtesy: Calgary Board of Education

Phyllis Weston taught English at Crescent Heights High School in Calgary. In 1961, when I was in Grade 11, I enrolled in her creative writing class. That one elective shaped my future career as a writer, and the lessons I learned from Miss Weston contributed to such success as I have enjoyed in ways that I could never have imagined all those years ago. During our year together she worked a kind of teaching magic that is still a mystery to me.

Miss Weston's magic involved much hard work both for her and her twenty-five students. She prepared assignments which required us to write volumes. This meant that she, in turn, marked volumes. Miss Weston did this quickly, meticulously and with uncommon perception—all qualities of good editing that I have come to value for their rarity in my professional world. The magic came as we laboured away at our daily writing assignments. I do not know how she worked her spells, but one day I was a kid who liked writing and the next I was a kid who could write. My ten months with Miss Weston may not have turned me into a prose stylist but at least I could write respectable sentences and string enough of them together to make an article or story or script. In other words, Miss Weston prepared me for a profession.

Over the years I have written for television, newspapers, film and magazines. At present, I write novels. I had to develop new skills and techniques in order to work in such varied fields, but the basic principles I have applied to all of them I learned in Miss Weston's class. She taught me to approach the work, the craft, and the art of writing in a disciplined and self-critical manner. She taught me that I might ignore the rules of grammar if I chose, but I remained ignorant of them at my peril. She taught me the inestimable value of a good editor. She taught me to love words, to respect their power and to use them honestly.

A number of years ago, I wrote a letter to Miss Weston to thank her for what she had given to me. It was my first and only letter of its kind, but I thought then, and still do, that the gift of a profession is worth thanks. For me writing has been not simply a source of remuneration but of great personal satisfaction and happiness. It is a remarkable thing for one teacher in one year of one class to have such an influence on a student's life.

We Need More Women in Science

by Susan Kent-Davidson

Eva Jagoe
Viscount Bennett School, Calgary

I remember best three women from my six years at Viscount Bennett Junior/Senior High. Two of them were so easy to love and admire: Marilyn Perkins, my English teacher and our choir leader, and Dorothy Hawley, our French teacher.

But Miss Jagoe—Eva Jagoe had three strikes against her if you were a teenaged girl in 1961. She taught math. She was the vice-principal. And she made no concessions on the lovability front.

She was stern. She was brilliant, rigorous, and not at all bothered by having to play bad cop to our sweet Principal Hugh Bryan's good cop. I sometimes felt that she was angry at us, especially at the girls, for falling the way we did for a culture of popularity and easy pleasures.

Although math scared me then and still does, I had a sneaky appreciation of its beauty. Only once in my life have I thrown a book at a wall, and it was a Grade 12 math book, in a moment of sudden revelation of where I had gone wrong.

Even in those days, I knew that I came from literature, but for a brief time with Miss Jagoe, I glimpsed the connections between numbers and rhythm, science and art. To my horror, she noticed. One day out of the blue, it came: "Susan, we need more women in science." She had just stopped me in the hall, days before graduation, stared at me, and delivered that line.

I failed her, of course, and she must have known that I would, that it was still too early for the full crusade against feminine stereotypes. I love the vocation that I had already chosen then, but Miss Jagoe and her challenge comes back to me sometimes when I think of what was about to happen to women of my age and the generations to follow.

No credit to me, but I now have a step-daughter who is a professor of math and physics. I'm sure that she and her sisters in science have had to fight a few of the same battles against stereotypes that had Miss Jagoe's jaw set so firm and fierce. But they are living out her dream for younger women, and I like to imagine that the thought of them would make her smile.

Math Was a Secret Weapon

by Murray Smith

Stan Mallet
Central Junior High School, Red Deer

It's really a tossup determining who made the most impact in Grade 9 at Central Junior High School in Red Deer in 1961 on an impressionable student just entering his teenage years. Unfortunately for me, I was more known for my overall impatience at structure and classroom discipline, than for my razor-sharp, rapier-like mind (that I knew I had . . . but could not understand why no teacher had discovered this reservoir of brilliance). Miss Florence Murray—a quintessential English grammar teacher, known for her sharp words of criticism to all within the hearing distance of an island foghorn—was a legendary terror of the hallways of Central Junior High. Miss Murray ensured, demanded, proper conduct, good use of manners, and good study habits. The other choice: Mr. Stan Mallet, an upright, suit-wearing, stern-talking math teacher, who brooked no fools, was the first teacher I encountered who treated students as mature people, able to make good and bad decisions, know the difference, and suffer the consequence.

The nod has to go to Mr. Mallet. He was the first person I had ever met who multiplied double and triple digit numbers in his head. Wow, what strength thought I, who was always looking for a way to avoid putting pen to paper and conducting laborious math extensions. Having impressed myself, and other spellbound classmates, continually over the first three months of class, we finally summoned the nerve to ask how he did it.

I remember him looking at us with some suspicion and a mirthful smile. It was easy he said: all that was required was knowledge of the times table up to twelve times twelve (144, right? ten times eleven, 110?) and the square table up to twenty five times twenty five (625?). This became our passion for the balance of the school year and one would hear shouts across playgrounds and at lunch hours: eleven times eleven (121), thirteen times thirteen (169) and so on. Many hours were spent outside of the classroom honing our talent. This wasn't home-work, this was learning a new secret weapon, a kind of mathematical finesse known only to a certain elite; we were part of a select group. We were *special!* Net effect—Mr. Mallet graduated a class full of kids who saw math as their pas-sion and recognized the natural beauty, congruence, uniformity of numbers, and the satisfaction of having met a challenge.

I still do it today, trying to beat the cash register at Sears and the Bay. Adding the GST in a sales tax free Alberta is my only anchor. Thank you Mr. Mallet for a lifetime gift.

A Life Beyond the Classroom Walls

by Myrna Kostash

Margaret (Hardy) Simpson
Ross Sheppard (Composite) High School, Edmonton

As a high school student, I was serious and earnest and always wanted to please my teachers, but it wasn't until I had Miss Hardy as my French teacher that I finally had a teacher I wanted to *be* like.

This was at Ross Sheppard CHS in Edmonton in 1961 and 1962 when classes were still streamed. My class was the "brain" class and the intellectual competitiveness was fierce. But Miss Hardy (later Mrs. Simpson) operated from the basic principle, "Show me. You all think you're so smart? Show me."

And so I found myself desperate for her approval and nothing was so terrifying as to make her mad. I was traumatized for weeks by her swift and brutal kick at the wastepaper basket by her desk when somebody's stupidity—surely not mine!—irritated her one day. By the same token, nothing was as invigorating as her pleasure in our work, and I became a very good French language student indeed.

But it was Miss Hardy the person, the character, who fascinated me. It was terribly intriguing that she was the daughter of Dr. W.G. Hardy, a classics professor at the University of Alberta, who had a sideline in writing bodice-rippers about ancient Rome. She was not glamorous physically, with her fuzzy hair, her boxy suits and her way of standing with legs apart, hands behind her back, like a sergeant-major reviewing the woebegone troops. But she zinged with infectious energy and enthusiasm which, I now see from long retrospection, was really passion for her own life. And in the milieu of a French language class, this meant her life á la française.

Week after week, I would sit spellbound by her "show and tell" about France. This is how I fell in love with Gerard Phillippe, the dark-eyed, supple-bodied stage and cinema actor who had died much too young only a couple of years earlier, when Miss Hardy held up an issue of *Paris Match* with pages of photographs of his life and career. This is how I learned all the words to *La Mer* and *Feuilles Mortes* when Miss Hardy brought in a portable record-player and her Charles Trenet and Yves Montand albums; music she herself had learned to love when she lived in Paris. This is how I knew that students in France sang a silly ditty we all then proceeded to learn: *J'aime maman, j'aime papa, j'aime ma petite soeur, mon petit frère et son grand éléphant*. This is how I knew that in Paris at the break of dawn you could go to the huge marketplace known as Les Halles and have a bowl of onion soup after a night of too much wine.

I no longer remember the details of Miss Hardy's Paris sojourn—was she at the Sorbonne or only a summer tourist? I have never lived in Paris, but the important message I took away from her was that there was a life out there— beyond the classroom walls—to live with music, art, and beauty, a secret held within *la langue française* but available to anyone with *joie de vivre*.

A Force to be Reckoned With

by Donna Lea Anderson

Gladys Lovegrove
Glendale Elementary School, Calgary

Imagine a towering teacher with blazing eyes, pointing a sinewy finger and exclaiming, "You there!" The students at Glendale Elementary trembled and fell into line when Gladys Lovegrove ruled with her iron digit. But it is not her indomitable presence that I remember most vividly.

Yes, we studied math and science, social studies and language. But somehow she also found the time and energy to provide the enrichment that, for many of us, would not have been available during the often unimaginative curricula of the 1960s.

Each year at Christmas time we began to prepare a nativity panto consisting of carols, artistic sets, imaginative costumes, and dialogue fit for royalty. The amount of time and energy expended on this one project alone would have daunted another teacher.

We went on nature walks in the country to learn to identify dozens of wild flowers. She taught us to read music so proficiently that we became an orchestral accompaniment to the weekly Friday morning assemblies. Our musical education grew to enormous proportions in the spring when she helped us to prepare for the Kiwanis Music Festival—an orchestra, duets and trios, choir and elocution. When we studied art, she chose the best projects to be entered in the Calgary Exhibition and Stampede school art contest. A great many of us were proud to display our prize ribbons and to enjoy the meagre cash prizes that accompanied them.

Classic civilizations were her particular favourites—Greece, Rome, the Aztecs, Incans, Mayans. All of these people and their achievements became vividly alive through her imaginative descriptions and projects.

We even went on field trips! How many students of the school system of that time can say that they actually went anywhere during school hours? We went on many. When replicas of the Crown Jewels were displayed at a local mall, we went to gaze in awe at them, of course, only after we had studied their significance and history. My first introduction to symphony was a school trip to the newly-constructed Jubilee Auditorium for a special presentation by the fledgling Calgary Symphony Orchestra.

Perhaps it was sheer strength of will which earned her a place on the administration of our school. Imagine a woman in a supervisory role! What a superior teacher she must have been to earn that spot! We all knew that only a man could be a principal, but we also knew who the boss in our school was. Without even giving it much thought, she had been a feminist inspiration to the girls.

Like a sponge, for two years, I soaked up the knowledge, ideas and skills which she imparted. And as the years passed I often found myself remembering or reciting some kernel of wisdom she had taught. Those seeds she had sown in my fantasies brought me to visit interesting countries and to read about many more. To her I owe my good grammar, my elocution and my unquenchable thirst for knowledge. Her dedication and inspiration are probably what lay at the bottom of my decision to become a teacher.

Ironically, when I finished university and first began my working career in a bank, Gladys Lovegrove was one of the customers. She was petite and silver-haired, but I could still feel her formidable aura. She was truly the epitome of what a teacher should be.

Thanks Mrs. Yellow

by Rob Cowie

Mary Roelofs
Barons Consolidated School, Barons

I can still remember my first day of Grade 1 at Barons Consolidated School in September 1962. My mom delivered me to the door of the room where we were met by what I considered to be a very tall woman in a bright yellow dress. "Hello, my name is Mrs. Roelofs, but if you can't remember that, you can call me by the colour of my dress. Today you can call me Mrs. Yellow."

I remember thinking to myself, "That seems kind of odd; I won't need to do that—surely I can remember this lady's name." I was immediately struck by her presence, her business-like approach and as each of us was dropped off, we were given a picture of a large apple and a red wax crayon. "I want you to colour that apple as red as you possibly can," were her instructions. "Don't stop until it's bright, bright red!"

As Mom left, I took my place at what I considered to be a large table at the back of the room where others were already hard at work producing the reddest apples they could manufacture. Mrs. Roelofs went back to welcoming the many students arriving with their parents. I knew some of the kids, but many were new to me and I remember being impressed with the industrious nature of most and even more intimidated with the quality of their colouring. It was apparent to me that I would need to improve my diligence with such tasks if I were to keep up with this bunch. Many of the apples, in deep, bright red, put mine to shame, as my creation was a shaded red that could only be described as pale. When I presented my apple it was obvious to me that "Mrs. Yellow" was not impressed. As I recall, I never did produce the hue she was looking for.

As was, and still is the case in many rural Alberta schools, Mrs. Roelofs' classroom was a Grade 1/2 split and I had the great fortune of being in her room for both of my first two years in school. I now realize that during that time I had the great fortune of learning to read, spell, understand numbers and grow as a child in a learning environment second to none. I had the privilege of beginning my public schooling with a teacher who believed in teaching the basic curriculum and did it well.

I also had many opportunities to develop my skills in the arts. From that first fall until the spring of '64 when I completed Grade 2, we were often planning, rehearsing and performing many plays, songs and/or poems that were presented at school Christmas pageants, special parent visit days and community events. With her strong hands at the keys of the piano and our young voices on stage, we produced many memorable moments for parents and ourselves alike. Now as I enjoy countless hours rehearsing and performing with an adult amateur theatre group, I often reflect upon the great start I had. It is obvious to me now that she believed in educating the entire child and with her penchant for music and the arts, she engaged us in learning that exposed us to the full range of opportunity. I will be eternally grateful to her for that.

It occurs to me now that Mrs. Roelofs must have become particularly attached to our class. Indicative of that attachment is the story she wrote and included in our report cards at the end of our Grade 2 year. As a work of literature, it was not incredibly awe-inspiring but to a group of 8-year-olds, it was a treasure. This was my first introduction to a genre that has been standard fare at many graduations over the years: the "prophecy". In her story, Mrs. Roelofs described a return to the Barons area after retirement where many years have passed and she discovers the entire class has grown up to become a group of fine adults engaged in a wide variety of occupations and lifestyles.

I shall never forget the paragraph in the middle of the piece that begins, "We then went up to Vulcan where we found Robert, a dentist, and he told us of . . ." It didn't strike me then as it does now but she was making a statement about me and what she felt I might be capable of becoming and accomplishing. It's a statement that will remain with me always.

Since that time, I have often reflected upon Mrs. R. and the many good times I enjoyed in her classroom. It occurs to me that maybe she knew something I didn't or nobody else could. I did not become a dentist, as she predicted, but I currently am principal at County Central High School in Vulcan. I often wonder what Mrs. Mary Roelofs would say if she could see me now. I know what I would say to her: "Thanks Mrs. Yellow—you were great!"

He Believed We Were Meant for Greatness

by Melanie Robinson

Bruce Honert
Central Elementary School, Lethbridge

The obituary read: *"Dr. Bruce Carlton Honert of Red Deer passed away at the Red Deer Regional Hospital on Tuesday, August 6, 2002, at the age of 69 years, as the result of a long battle with cancer . . . Bruce was very much a 'people person' with a phenomenal memory for names and faces . . . He was a dedicated educator and a proud Canadian . . . He will be much missed by all who knew him."*

I wept as I read it. It was Thursday and I was two days too late to tell him how much he meant to me. It wasn't that he didn't know, really. Since I was a kid of 10 sitting in his class, I credited Mr. Honert with knowing almost everything. But I'd travelled back to Alberta to tell him again.

Here I was, a woman of 50, a principal of an elementary school in Vancouver, deeply moved at this loss. My husband consoled me as I poured out some of the stories of this incredible teacher who powerfully impacted my life.

September—Grade 5—a skinny little Lethbridge kid terrified at having a "man-teacher". By the second day of school, this guy with big ears and a goofy sense of humour had won my heart. In October, my dad passed away, and Bruce Honert quietly became my guardian angel. Without any noticeable change toward me, he was ever watchful. At recess one day, he kept me in briefly. "I saw an expression of pain on your face when I said that"—a reference to a joke he had made about dads—"and I think I was not being as sensitive as I should have been. I'm sorry."

Years later, at Simon Fraser University, I read *Teaching As A Subversive Activity*. It was Honert all the way.

When the principal told him that science was to happen only *in* the classroom with a textbook, paper and pencil, Mr. Honert got permission from our parents to meet us Saturday mornings in the coulees surrounding Lethbridge. We observed and collected flora and fauna there, and saw the dusty, brown hills with new eyes as an amazing ecosystem on our doorstep.

He read aloud each day after lunch. In the middle of *The Incredible Journey*, with each child hanging on every word, the principal came into the room. He told Honert this was a waste of our time. We should be reading for ourselves. Mr. Honert no longer read aloud but, instead, walked us to the public library after school the next day. He made sure we all had a library card and knew how to find the book we wanted. We learned how to put a book on reserve. Each kid put a reserve on *The Incredible Journey*.

When Mr. Honert walked across the school grounds, every child called out hello. Bruce was able to answer each one by name. He knew all about us. He believed we were meant for greatness. Near the end of Grade 6, Mr. Honert organized groups in fours and took us after school—group by group—to the Lethbridge College campus. We walked the broad hallways while he described the exciting courses available: chemistry, biology, sociology, psychology. The tour completed, we sipped coke in the college cafeteria, with Mr. Honert and all the cool campus crowd. Six years later, I was a charter student at the University of Lethbridge.

I went off to high school as Honert went off to be superintendent in Peace River and, later, an Alberta Ministry of Education consultant. But he didn't forget about me. Whenever he could, he would check in, guiding me to do something important. He corrected my mother who thought I was a dreamer—he said I should be focused on a master's degree. I did just that with a master's degree in education.

Of course, I became a teacher. I wanted to be who Bruce Honert was for me. Children need to be seen and heard; to have an adult believe in them, guiding them through the tough stuff.

I wanted to tell Mr. Honert just one more time: he was that unforgettable teacher who I daily aspire to be.

You're a Writer

by Betty Jane Hegerat

Mary Wynne Ashford
Bonnie Doon Composite High School, Edmonton

In 1963 my family moved from Camrose to Edmonton. I landed, terrified, at Bonnie Doon Composite, a high school three times the size of the one I had been attending. I was assigned to Mrs. Ashford's homeroom. She was also my English 10 teacher; a vivacious young woman with a passion for language and an enthusiasm for life's possibilities which she shared eloquently.

While I was probably one of the most awkward and obviously miserable young women to land in Mrs. Ashford's classroom that year, I was an honour student, and English was my strongest subject. I was a quiet observer, but in my head I narrated a thousand adventures. One of my first assignments was to write a story, a poem, something from personal experience. I don't remember what I wrote, but something about that bubbly young woman made me trust her enough to let the rambling in my head spill onto the paper. The day after I turned in the first assignment, she looked up when I entered the classroom, smiled and walked across to my desk.

"You're a writer," she said. "What are you going to do about that?"

I went red-faced, and stammered.

"I want you to meet my mother," she said. "She's a writer too and she's just down the hall."

By the next year, Mrs. Ashford was gone (she was back in university studying medicine—pursuing the next dream), but her mother, Mrs. Moar, was my English teacher. My first creative writing assignment came back riddled with red and a note on the bottom: Come see me about this. Mortified, I crept back to her classroom at the end of the day.

"This is a wonderful story," she said. "Now let me tell you what these red marks mean and why I made them and then you'll rewrite it and send it away." Rewrite I did, and at Mrs. Moar's insistence, I sent the story to the *Edmonton*

Journal's Third Column. It was published and I received the hefty payment of fifteen dollars. The story also won an Honourable Mention in the Canadian Women's Press Club awards. When the Edmonton chapter of the CWPC invited me to be a guest at their dinner meeting, Mrs. Moar picked me up, and mothered me through the evening.

My dream of being a writer went on ice for twenty-five years. Practicality prevailed. I completed a BA and an MSW and went on to a career in social work. But the story tapes continued to roll in my head.

Mrs. Ashford's name suddenly appeared in the mid-eighties in a magazine article about Peter Gzowski's fiftieth birthday. He'd been asked to name six women with whom he would like to share that celebration. Dr. Mary Wynne Ashford was one of his choices. She was the co-president of International Physicians for the Prevention of Nuclear War.

On my forty-fifth birthday in 1993, a good friend asked what I had dreamed of doing but had yet to pursue. I thought for a moment about making excuses. But in that moment I also remembered Mrs. Ashford and her endorsement, "You're a writer. What are you going to do about that?"

I registered for a creative writing course, and another and another. I am now a writer. My first novel will be published in 2006. I have had stories published in fine literary magazines and broadcast on CBC radio.

In October, 2004, Dr. Mary Wynne Ashford was in Calgary to deliver the Elizabeth Flagler Memorial Award. If I'd known at the time, I would have attended so that I could tell her that she and her mother gave me an ember that I carried with me for twenty-five years. When the time was finally right, I was able to fan it into flame. I am so grateful.

When the Stars Aligned Themselves

by Jean Filewych

Sister Margaret Rose (Theresa Ford)
Archbishop O'Leary High School, Edmonton

Archbishop O'Leary HS Choir. Sister Margaret Rose and Jean (2nd row, 2nd on the left).
Courtesy: Jean Filewych

For most, a teacher's influence is rarely harmful, nor spectacularly life-changing. Every once in a while, if we are lucky, the stars in the heavens align themselves and we get *the* teacher we never forget.

My stars aligned themselves favourably in my Grade 12 year in 1963 at Archbishop O'Leary High School in Edmonton. You could not miss her. The reason you could not miss her was because she was a nun. Put a tall, sturdy woman in a severe, imposing habit and the effect was well, *imposing.* I was fascinated by the habit: it was black and white (typical of the day). Her face was jolly and constantly on the verge of a raucous laugh. A black veil adorned her head; this large bib-like piece covered her chest, from which flowed a black robe with its classic rosary beads looped and clicking softly as she moved. The clothing seemed to be trying too hard to contain a woman and not succeeding very well. Each day she would stand at the classroom door with her arms folded over her breasts holding down the white breastplate of her habit. I now wonder why she stood there every day—school policy or trendy teaching pedagogy? Or did she just want to greet us?

Her class was pure magic. She did what only good teachers can do. She lifted the material *off* the page. I wish I could tell you how. I cannot. And the irony is that the only real content I recall her teaching is *Hamlet*. I could not wait to get to class. And then she showed us the Christopher Plummer version of the play and I was hooked. Prince Hamlet took root in my psyche and he has never left.

She took us into her confidence as her equals and led us through what the text revealed in all its complexities. When we got to know her better, we tentatively asked questions we were curious about. Why had she become a nun, we wanted to know? She said it was because she had red hair: not high currency for marriage, she teased. From that day forth, I strained to see an errant red hair peeking from her headdress.

She was an effective teacher. But it did not end here. She was the director of the glee club. And really she was choreographer and conductor and stage director and costume and set designer. She did it all. The school put on these amazing concerts, quite professional really. And they spoke to me as profoundly as did *Hamlet*. Who better to coach us to sing with gusto "I'm gonna wash that man right out of my hair?" or the sweet innocent lyrics of "Daisy, Daisy, I'm half crazy all for the love of you." I could in some perverse yet harmless way, snub my nose at the more popular and beautiful girls who actually got dates or be less self-conscious about my ethnic roots by entering into the great epics we sang: I was on the high seas or at the centre of a love story . . . oh, how rich my life was on the risers in the gym in front of that nun waving her hands with her bib going up and down with every beat.

Probably the most direct effect Sister Margaret Rose had on me came out of the blue. After one particular assignment, she asked if she might send my essay off to an essay contest. I still remember the feeling of pride and excitement washing over me. She thought I could write, she thought I could write I whispered all the way home. It was like a present and I could open it over and over again. And I did. I hardly remember whether or not I won the contest. It did not matter. The seed had been planted: she thought I could write.

I believe that Sister Margaret Rose was a great teacher because she recognized and legitimized in her students *what was already there*. She sensed my love of words and responded. She sensed my teenage awkwardness and responded. She sensed my yearnings for adventure and responded. No small feat, considering I never overtly revealed this inner trembling. She nurtured who I was and that led directly to who I became: an English teacher, a member of a choir still on the high seas or in the middle of an epic tale. My sense of adventure I surely needed in my own epic: my life.

She encountered her own epic battle: she courageously battled Parkinson's disease. I visited Sister, now Theresa Ford, living in Windsor, Ontario, and corresponded with her until the end of her life. I discovered how many, many lives she had touched. One of the main activities of her day was answering mail she received from her former Alberta students. When we went out for dinner, she still commanded attention, even without the habit, because now she had a matching cane for every outfit; she was not letting the monster Parkinson's make a mockery of her or shrivel up her soul. She may have needed help walking, but the help would be stylish and dramatic and dynamic . . . just like her teaching.

Cutting Class
by Robert Kim Greyson

Bill Dais
Fairview Elementary and Junior High School, Calgary

Teachers! As we go through our formative years—our guides, our nemeses, and our inspirations—are the many teachers we encounter along the way to adulthood. Sometimes we are pulled kicking and screaming down paths we do not want to go. Other times we are presented the unexpected.

My story takes place during my Grade 8 year (1966–1967) at Fairview Elementary and Junior High School in Calgary.

Mr. Dais was my homeroom teacher, my science teacher and my basketball coach. He was young, enthusiastic and really knew how to handle and reach Grade 8 students. We looked forward to his classes and his creative way of teaching the subject.

I have never been very good at science; this one year though, Mr. Dais brought science to life for me. He began the year with zoology, something I truly loved and because of that I studied hard and pulled the highest mark in the class.

Unfortunately, because of that exam, I was labelled the "science guru" and whenever anyone had a problem in science they came to me. Luckily I returned to my old ways the next year.

But, that is not the story. As we all know, everyone tries skipping class at one time or another. My best friend Tom and I decided to cut a Wednesday afternoon class to go downtown to see the Dean Martin movie, *Murderer's Row*, at the now extinct Palace Theatre. We hid in the balcony and watched with guilty delight as Matt Helm saved the world once more.

After the movie—reality set in. I had to get my homework otherwise my mother would ask me where it was. We caught the bus home, Tom got off at our home stop and I went back to school. I went to my homeroom to pick up my stuff. The door was locked. Since I had recently graduated from Lock

Picking 101, I got into my classroom. I grabbed my homework from my desk and opened the door to leave. Standing there was Mr. Dais, with his key in his hand, ready to open the door. We looked at each other in surprise. *I'm dead*, I thought to myself. I'd skipped his last period science class and had broken into his classroom. Detention or worse here I come.

Something strange happened at that moment. Instead of reading me the riot act and marching me down to the principal's office, Mr. Dais said to me, "Kim I see you have your homework. Did you forget that we have a basketball game in ten minutes? Hustle your butt to the changing room and get changed and be ready to play."

Without a word, I put my homework into my locker and ran to the changing room. We won the game and I even scored my first basket of the year.

Mr. Dais did not phone home or tell the office about my escapades. Instead, he told my homeroom class that if we wanted to skip one of his classes for something important, just let him know. He was the master of reverse psychology.

I learned my lesson about cutting class. In fact, I never skipped a class again until my university days. My friend Tom, on the other hand, cut class the very next week, was caught and ended up with a two week detention.

It is simple situations like this, when teachers like Mr. Dais know instinctively how to handle a moment that can either go down in flames or leave a heart-warming memory.

Like Mr. Dais I became a teacher. I have taught students from Grades 1 to 12 for the past twenty-four years. Many is the time I have had to deal with student moments. When these moments are difficult I often think, "How would Mr. Dais have handled this problem?"

Hopefully I have followed in Mr. Dais' footsteps and have left a heart-warming memory with some of my students. Mr. Dais, wherever you are, thanks for showing me the way!

Inspiring Words, Inspiring History

by Faye Reineberg Holt

Peter Chitrenky
William Hay Composite High School, Stettler

When I was attending William Hay Composite High School in Stettler, I never dreamed of writing short stories, poetry, articles and ten books of regional history. I liked school but friends were my focus. Then in 1966 and 1967, I had an exceptional teacher who inspired my love of literature and history.

In Grade 10 and 11, English was split into literature and language classes. Mr. Peter Chitrenky taught Literature 11 and Literature 21, but he was also my teacher for Social 30. Eventually, words and history would become the stuff of life for me, and love of those subjects began with Mr. Chitrenky.

Peter Chitrenky and Faye Reineberg Holt.
Courtesy: Faye Reineberg Holt

I vividly remember him reading aloud, his voice booming out some of the world's greatest poetry. The ideas were important, but in the sound, rhythms and nuances were other dimensions to appreciate. Mr. Chitrenky asked us read aloud, too, and I was always nervous, but when I taught high school English years later and, today, when I read to audiences, I know where I learned the confidence to add my voice to the voices of others.

In Mr. Chitrenkey's Lit 21, we were introduced to great literature, but there was history, too. We discovered that the time-frame and culture had an impact on how writers *felt* and saw the world. As well, their personal experiences had an impact on their words.

In Social 30, once again, people's experiences mattered. We studied both world wars and their effect on Canada. Events and concepts were part of the curriculum, but Mr. Chitrenky made the people and events come alive. While serving in the infantry during the Second World War, Mr. Chitrenky had been in Britain and continental Europe. During demobilization, he was in Germany, and his stories made the war significant to students growing up in the flower-power, anti-war culture of the Sixties and early Seventies.

Ahead of his time, he used film as well as books for teaching materials. We watched the *Canada at War* series, and lagging attention was never a good idea. Films weren't just something to pass the time with impatient adolescents. Questions followed—ones we were expected to *think* about—rather than parrot a memorized answer. Yet, memorization was valued, too. And years later, when I would quote passages of Shakespeare by heart to students, I realized I had developed a respect for what memory might add to our lives.

Mr. Chitrenky enjoyed the interaction with students and chose the classroom. He knew we considered ourselves adults, and he treated us as young adults. His methods were both traditional and contemporary. When he had a question and called your last name, you sat to attention. But he smiled often and joked and laughed with us, too. He could be lenient when we turned around to talk to the student behind us. But, we were never confused. The bell rang or his pointer banged on his desk, and the room was silent—until we were expected to add out two cents about history, ideas and literature.

Was he a great teacher only for students who liked academic subjects? No. In night school, he taught English as a second language, and today, he remembers how grateful those students were. There, he also taught fellows upgrading their steam tickets. He admitted he knew nothing about steam. They knew steam. He knew the math involved, and his students were proud to have achieved the equivalent of Math 30.

Personally, I am grateful he conveyed the magic of literature, the importance of history, and the link between personal stories, history and literature. Thank you, Mr. Chitrenky. May I somehow convey to others the same life-changing lessons you taught me.

Passion for Compassion

by Trudy Sribney

Nellie Sribney
St. Mary's Elementary School, Vegreville

My most influential and unforgettable teacher was my Grade 2 teacher. It is her everyday *passion for compassion* that comes to mind when I think of her. She often referred to my classmates and me as her special "family of sweethearts".

Each morning she welcomed us with a warm embrace and assured us that we would experience a beautiful day in our "colourful classroom world". Class began with a song; with out-stretched arms in a gesture of love, she would sing:

> *Good morning to you!*
> *Good morning I say!*
> *Whatever the weather,*
> *We'll make it together,*
> *A beautiful day*

With an exchange of smiles, we sang back:

> *Let us smile when we say "Good Morning",*
> *For a smile makes our faces bright!*
> *Let us smile when we say "Good Morning",*
> *For a smile starts the day off right!*

Yes, we had "Classroom Rules"; one posted on the wall was our "Golden Rule". It read: "DO UNTO OTHERS as YOU would have them DO UNTO YOU!" This simple rule encouraged us to take responsibility for our own actions. Our "serious" Grade 2 dilemmas (like, who pinched who first?) were always kindly addressed. She was a great listener and typically her resolve was to have those involved agree to a compromise. She reminded us to focus on the "Golden Rule" to assist us in solving our differences.

My Grade 2 teacher was not one to display "Star Charts" that compared pupils' abilities. Regardless of mistakes, all completed assignments were stamped with a star for doing our best. For working quietly, we were rewarded with surprise classroom "chit-chat breaks".

My Grade 2 teacher also had a passion for creativity in her teaching techniques. She had a flair for making learning the basic 3R's fun! She inspired us to use our imagination and express our feelings freely through writing, art, drama, and song. To this day, I insist that Halloweeners sing me a song before I hand out treats. If they don't know one, then I sing to them one of the several songs I learned in Grade 2. (Admittedly, I am now 44.)

Parents (or other loved ones) received keepsake letters of appreciation and humour on Mother's Day and Father's Day written by us. When the Honourable Don Mazankowski was honoured for twenty years of service as the Member of Parliament for Vegreville, his son Greg (my Grade 2 classmate), surprised his father by reading the letter he had written to Don twenty years earlier. My teacher, who attended the celebration, said it was a beautiful tribute of love that brought on both tears and laughter! To this day, I have the letters written to my mother and father that were inspired by my teacher. They are my most priceless treasure.

Field trips were abundant! Reflecting on them, they were simple, yet perfect for us 7-year-olds. A tour to a local hatchery landed our class with a duckling to care for. My teacher endured several days of quacking in the corner of our classroom until it went to her parents' farm where it lived happily ever after!

Another memorable field trip shared with my 1967–68 class was a year-end school picnic in our teacher's yard. As a class, we walked with her across a meadow, looking and listening for signs of spring. Every trip outside of the classroom was a learning experience. Science was made to be fun! Arriving at her home, there was a big friendly chef (her husband) ready to serve us barbequed hot dogs and treats of all kinds! Exploring inside her home was a great adventure! This teacher treated all her classes of students throughout the years to a special year-end picnic at her home until her retirement in 1995.

My most memorable and influential teacher, is none other than . . . Mrs. Nellie Sribney, my dear mom.

The Gala
by Clem Martini

Lois Vance

R.B. Bennett Elementary School, Calgary

In 1967 I was both deranged and in Grade 5 which made everything difficult. It wasn't entirely my fault. The previous year I had been enrolled in a class that had—for reasons I still cannot fully fathom—been evenly divided between what was then termed the "slow learning" Grade 5s and the "advanced" Grade 4s. If this strategy was meant to inspire the Grade 5s to greater and more assiduous academic efforts, it was an utter failure. If it was meant to crush the spirit of the bookish Grade 4s and make us feel that our education was a hollow sham, learning was a joke and existence itself was dangerously capricious, it was a triumph.

I spent my entire Grade 4 term facing down my surly rightfully resentful Grade 5 peers and trying to comprehend our bored, bitter teacher. She was from Texas. She was a devout evangelist. She supplemented our admittedly impoverished curriculum with an ad hoc program of enrichment that consisted primarily of lengthy Bible study and improvised lectures on why Indians didn't deserve reserves and the Black Panthers were common criminals. On good days she rewarded us by reading aloud from a seemingly endless supply of folksy animal stories that almost always ended with the animal protagonist getting shot.

I spent the dusty summer after my disastrous Grade 4 in recovery. I followed the demonstrations and upheavals that were happening in universities all over North America. I was pretty sure that institutional education was a sham and in any case I was certain that my Grade 4 year had been a travesty. What I'm trying to say is I entered Grade 5 with low expectations.

Mrs. Vance, my Grade 5 teacher, changed all that. She was thin, pale-skinned, a little owlish and soft spoken. I believe she had some kind of eye disorder because she wore special sunglasses even inside. Other teachers had, in the past, been very clear about the kinds of distinctions we were to expect. Classes were organized in a hierarchical fashion according to academic achievement: high-achieving students sat in the respected Blue Birds' rows, poorer students in the despised Jays'.

Mrs. Vance had no time for that sort of thing. In her class you sat where you elected to sit. She was endlessly patient with everyone and especially, I believe, with me. When I raged that the "system" was unfair, she responded by quietly placing a student complaint box on the wall which I promptly put to good use. The curriculum was lame, I objected. The education system didn't reward intellectual curiosity. History, as taught, was racist and fraught with glaring omissions. There were social inequities between wealthy and poor students that our school didn't address and, in fact, encouraged. She didn't patronize me. She didn't lead me to believe that things would suddenly get better. Instead she discussed each complaint with me and genuinely tried to find solutions with uneven success. We never fully solved the social inequities thing—she tactfully suggested that might be something I might be able to tackle when I grew older.

When the school year ended, other teachers threw parties that generally consisted of a hot and sticky hour-long bus ride to the zoo, a picnic of soggy egg-salad sandwiches on an arid patch of brittle grass beside the llamas, followed by a short but desperate bout of heat stroke and salmonella. Instead, our Mrs. Vance gallantly offered to host a year-end gala in the gym, at night. At night! No one held year end parties at night—except adults. The symbolism was not lost on us. We dressed up—and I believe we grew up—for that event.

We organized our year-end party down to the very last detail. We were courteous to one another. We read from flowery speeches we had prepared for her. It was the perfect conclusion to a year that had been made bearable largely because of her wit and patience. Maybe her glasses were special because she definitely was endowed with superior vision. She saw us. She saw our potential. She was somehow able to sense a time, in the not so distant future, beyond our inflammatory adolescent rhetoric and hysteria, to a place when we would become almost human. She valued us and she encouraged us to value ourselves. It was an important—perhaps the most important—lesson of my entire education.

Thank heavens for her.

Taking Small Steps
by Terrence Oster

George Dann
Western Canada High School, Calgary

George Dann taught Mathematics 30 to my university-bound Grade 12B class at Western Canada High School in Calgary in the late 1960s: that era of free love and exploratory learning. Mr. Dann did not stand for either. I was a nervous 17-year-old, cocky in my other classes, but lived in fear of mathematics and had only escaped from Math 20 with a 57 percent average. Hardly a sound background for the trials of Math 30 and the torments that I felt awaited me in Mr. Dann's class, because his classes were legendary in that school, and I had heard about them almost from the day that I had registered in Grade 10.

My first day confirmed that what I had heard was all true, and I sat in my seat cringing that day and for weeks after. He did have my attention, however, and I soon began to see the logic not only of mathematics but of the man as a teacher. He did not seriously expect his students to ever understand mathematics. He expected them to understand a system that would allow them to figure out mathematics, to make every student, in effect, his own teacher, so that he would understand not only mathematics but perhaps other aspects of life itself. His method then, was to teach a method, and I became intrigued by this.

Mr. Dann taught according to the following principles. First, the lessons were short. Although the period might have been forty-five minutes long, Mr. Dann could easily cover a dozen aspects of the curriculum in that time, spending only a few minutes on each. Second, the lessons were repetitive. If one did not understand some aspect of the previous lesson, not to worry, because Mr. Dann would present it again in a slightly different form, perhaps with different examples, the next day and maybe the day after that and maybe all year if necessary, always expanding and always developing his topics every so slightly. Third, Mr. Dann, by virtue of the previous two points, always took small steps. He did not cover in detail a huge portion of the curriculum at once, only to leave it and never to visit it until the year-end review, a common practice of other teachers. Fourth, Mr. Dann was a time-on-task dictator. From the minute he took attendance each day to the final bell, students were fully engaged in learning mathematics. Every minute was treated as though it was the minute that would make it possible for us to pass the departmental examination. Finally, and most importantly, Mr. Dann did not allow any student to fall behind. He would assign a problem on the blackboard, and two minutes later he would have toured the entire classroom of thirty students and seen who had succeeded and who had failed, and he would have corrected on their notebooks the mistakes of the students who had not got the answer right. So how was it possible for one teacher to mark thirty notebooks so quickly? He could mark them so quickly because few of his students ever got the answers wrong, He taught to be understood, not to confuse; for us to succeed, not to fail. We became confident mathematicians.

I passed the departmental examination with a 67 percent average, ten percent higher than I had received the previous year, and instead of failing Grade 12 miserably because of my aversion to mathematics, I was admitted to the University of Calgary. I never again used the mathematics that he taught me, but an unexpected thing happened. I became an elementary teacher, and I discovered that Mr. Dann's teaching system involving small steps, high time-on-task, constant repetition, and immediate feedback with reinforcement was adaptable to all instruction involving my first to sixth graders, and I used Mr. Dann's methods for years. Later, I would do five years of graduate school and become a school psychologist. What did I usually write somewhere on the evaluations I conducted on learning and behaviour disordered students? I recommended small steps, high time-on-task, constant repetition and immediate feedback with reinforcement.

I sometimes wonder about the lessons of life implicit in Mr. Dann's methods. I also wonder if I, as a teacher, was ever as good as George Dann, but I know the answer. There can be many students but only one master.

Dear Mrs. Major

by Michelle Crighton

Lorraine (RivaCambrin) Major
Central School, Lethbridge

It may seem strange that you are receiving this letter, but I have thought about sending it for a long time and decided the time was now. You may not even remember me, but I was a student in your Grade 3 class at Central School in 1969 and you were Miss RivaCambrin then. When writing this letter, I was a bit concerned that you might not still be teaching. It occurred to me that if I am 36 years older, then so are you. I did what I guessed to be the appropriate math and I am taking the chance you still are.

Have you ever wondered in your years of teaching if you have made a difference? Do you wonder if your students give you another thought after they leave your class for the last time? Well, that is the reason for my letter. We all spend twelve years in grade school and if we are lucky, we have one teacher who stands out in our minds; who challenges us years after they cease to have any direct influence over our lives. You were the first teacher to influence my views on education and my desire to pursue learning for the pure joy of it. I remember being a little apprehensive about starting Grade 3 in your class. Even then the students talked about what teachers they wanted and what teachers they didn't want. Most of them did not want to be in your class because they were scared of you. Most of my friends were scared of my mom too, so that did not really bother me. I did know that my mom had high expectations so I was a little apprehensive I would have to endure those same expectations at school as I did at home and that seemed like a tall order to one going into Grade 3. In the end, I was glad I would be entering your class and I never regretted it.

In your class, I was exposed to the French language for the first time and I loved the sound of it. I was not exposed to it again until Grade 8, but I continued with it until my first year of university when the time commitment was just too great to continue. I am obviously not fluent, but I am confident I will return to instruction in that area at some time in the future. I also remember having the opportunity to feel like we were part of the space program when we got to go up to the attic room in the school to glue bronze painted bottle caps onto the space ship if we finished our class work early. There are so many other things that often come to mind when I think back to that year. I recall your energy and enthusiasm for every subject matter we covered. It was always infectious. Most of all, I recall your efforts to find ways to reach all students and find the best way for them to learn what you needed to teach. That is a skill I did not often observe in later years in grade school or at any other level.

To this day, I am energized by the very opportunity to learn something new. I have recently returned to an old passion that I allowed a perceived lack of time to cause me to shelve for too many years—writing. So, if you wonder if you have made a difference in the lives of your former students, I can say most assuredly *yes* in my case. If you wonder if they ever give you a second thought after they leave your class for the last time, again, I can say in my case, more times and on more occasions than you could imagine.

I do have one confession to make. I don't know if you remember Judy Lee Rorick. She was pretty bright and had red hair. Anyway, she was first in the class that year and I was second. Well, that was a bit hard to take (I was competitive then and I am afraid to say I have not lost that competitive streak today). I did tell my mother that I really came first in the class, but you did not want to hurt Judy Lee's feelings. I am quite certain she found that as unbelievable as it sounds now, but she let me live with that one for as long as I wanted to.

I hope you are still enjoying teaching as much as you seemed to some thirty-six years ago. Thank you for the effort you exerted on my behalf so long ago.

The Desire to Do Good
by Edie Gegolick

Diane Cheremshynski
St. Martin's Catholic School, Vegreville

Fortunate to have had wonderful teachers throughout all my school years, there is definitely one who continues to stand out in my life. Mrs. Cheremshynski (fondly known as Mrs. "C") taught me in Grade 5 at St. Martin's Catholic School in Vegreville in 1969. Although she taught all the subjects in our class, math was definitely her favourite. She would dissect each problem into many simple steps and we quickly learned that "short cuts" were not in her math vocabulary. Documenting each step (one problem easily used up one and a half pages in our notebooks!) took its toll on our writing hands, but by year end, we were all pros at understanding the concepts of Grade 5 math. Without even being aware of it, we had been gently pushed to reach our fullest potential.

What forever sticks in my mind is that she was not only a superb teacher but a surrogate mother for many. Extremely intuitive to our needs, Mrs. Cheremshynski opened her heart to everyone and it was gratifying to see that emotionally insecure and troubled students were drawn to her kindness and warmth. A loving person, but firm and quick to discipline when warranted, her students clearly knew their boundaries and expectations and we all thrived under her guidance.

It is now thirty-six years later and I am proud to say that not only myself, but my own three boys, have experienced the joy of learning math through Mrs. Cheremshynski at St. Mary's High in Vegreville. (Two have since graduated.) There, she continues to teach math and carries on duties as vice-principal as well. Mrs. Cheremshynski wanted to make a difference in every child's life and the following story (as told by my 17-year-old son, Davin) clearly attests to that.

"Why can't *all* the teachers teach like Mrs. C, mom?" complained my son one day. As we spoke of the different teaching methods and the years of experience Mrs. C had, Davin shared his story of the day with me. (He usually comes home with many stories about the happenings in Mrs. C's class.) "You know, mom. Today we went to church for Ash Wednesday and there were a lot of kids who skipped out. But I'm in her homeroom class and I *knew* she would check up on us. There's *no way* I'd *ever* skip out of her class time! I'm scared of her!" (Many years later, Davin would come to realize that this "fright" was actually deep respect and the desire to do "good" in her eyes.) And sure enough, the following school day, Davin was approached by Mrs. C and asked if he had gone to church. Proudly, he said yes.

As he shared his story, my other son, Dayton (who has since graduated but also had Mrs. C for a math teacher in high school) piped up: "You know, mom. I remember one year when the school bus took us to church. Mrs. C was in the bus with us and we noticed one of her students walking on the sidewalk as we drove to church. We all realized he was probably skipping out and it was his unfortunate luck that we happened by at the same time. Mrs. C ordered the bus be stopped and quickly marched out to confront the unlucky chap. We crammed up against the windows of the bus, anticipating great entertainment. The student, noticing Mrs. C stalking towards him, turned tail and ran through someone's backyard with Mrs. C gaining on him and shouting for him to stop. Fear make feet nimble and they both disappeared behind the house. After agonizing minutes of waiting, we were finally rewarded with Mrs. C coming from the backyard, alone, but triumphantly carrying one of his running shoes. As she plopped the shoe on the seat beside her, she gloated, "I'll be seeing *him* at school tomorrow!"

Mrs. C's commitment to her students, and love for teaching is clearly indicated in the admiration and respect her students, past and present, have for her today. I'm truly lucky to call her one of my colleagues as I now work as secretary at St. Martin's Catholic School.

She Saw My Potential
by Linda Blasetti

Patricia Finestone
St. Francis High School, Calgary

Patricia M. Finestone (nee Biron) is a wife, a mother, a grandmother, a businesswoman and as importantly, she was my teacher. She is now my surrogate mother, my campaign manager, my mentor, my biggest fan, my toughest critic and I am proud to say, she is my friend.

Let me explain. Mrs. Finestone became my teacher in 1969 when I enrolled in the Beauty Culture program at St. Francis High School in Calgary. She saw the potential in me and worked hard to encourage me to see what she saw in me.

Now, Mrs. Finestone had three generations of one family in her life. Little did we know then what an enduring influence she would have for many years to come. My mother passed away in 1971 while I was in high school and as the oldest girl of eight children, the youngest child 7 years old at the time, I decided I should quit school and help my father raise our family.

Mrs. Finestone would have no part of my leaving school. She told my father that if she had to help me clean house on Saturday mornings, so that I could remain in school, then so be it. Time passed and Mrs. Finestone's untiring devotion to me and my family can never be measured. I completed my high school program, graduated with my Journeyman's Certificate and became a hairdresser, gainfully employed immediately upon graduation.

I became the owner of a beauty salon in 1980 which I sold to run for election as a Trustee for the Calgary Catholic School Board back in 1986. Mrs. Finestone declared herself my "campaign manager" and stuck with me through five campaigns over an eighteen year period, all of them successful campaigns.

She has been a sounding board, a confidant, and a fresh set of eyes through which to view issues as well as a provider of speaking material and quotable quotes over the years. Her English major has been well utilized! "Thank you" seems hardly sufficient to convey my appreciation for what she has done for me and my family, for the many lessons taught along my life journey and for the strength she has given me at difficult times in my life.

Mrs. Finestone has been this to many more students than me over the years. Her teaching career spans thirty-eight years, at all levels, including being a principal at the ripe age of 21! Mrs. Finestone developed and taught the first Beauty Culture program in the Calgary Catholic School District and thousands of graduates have benefited from this outstanding woman's lessons. She speaks often of one student or another, their accomplishments and the many gifts she gained in helping young people become productive contributors to a better society. Her motto, "Faith, Family, Education, Hard work and Loving Deeds" is engrained in so many of us, her former students.

Mrs. Finestone continues to give back to her community through her work with various charities across the province and country. Her passion for education is evident in her work with and for St. Mary's University College. Mrs. Finestone's legacy will live on long after she has left this world!

I am who I am today because of Mrs. Patricia Finestone, who saw my potential when I couldn't and wouldn't let go of her dreams and aspirations for me. Gracious, humble and kind, Patricia Finestone deserves our respect and gratitude for exemplifying the true characteristics of "TEACHER".

February Haiku

by Dave Jorgensen

Ken Marshall
Hardisty Junior High School, Edmonton

> *The skier dips his*
> *flashing blades into the snow*
> *and then he is gone*

Dear Mr. Marshall:

You won't remember this particular haiku any more, but in the winter of '69 at Hardisty Junior High School you were doing a poetry unit with us in Language Arts 8. We wrote, you wrote, we plastered poetry on the blackboards, the hallways—you even put some up in the glass of the office window. I'm not sure why, but you gave me a leftover Halloween caramel for this one, and I've never forgotten either the caramel or the poem.

You'll be happy to know that I've just come from the school playground where I herded a group of Grade 7s out the door, past the *swings and snowbound struggled spruce* (alliteration and seven syllables—get it?) We went up the sliding hill, looked southwest over the horizon towards Pigeon Lake, wondered at the different textures of clouds, then watched a bunch of boys on testosterone overload yell and slide down the berm on their backsides.

We made our way back inside, scrounged pens and paper, and then began to cackle and write. The ones who can't normally sit still began to scrawl, firing page after seventeen syllable page at each other. Others huddled in groups, pushing paper back and forth, whispering, "That's eight syllables, not seven!" After class, young basketball players, otherwise disinterested in the vagaries of figurative language, accosted me in the hallway with images of Canada geese in winged V's, rabbit turds in snow, cotton clouds against slate horizons.

It's February now, after teachers' convention, and it's a long haul from here to spring break, you'll remember. But we saw the sun today, giggled a whole lot, put pen to paper. I'll see this crowd again this afternoon, and we'll go to the computer lab and nail these things down in 36-point font, then we'll find bare corridor wherever we can and we'll paper these wintertime walls. Oh—and you'll be happy to know that I've got some leftover Christmas candy canes that'll get passed out, too. I mean, if part of beating the February greyness is a little literary endeavour, then a bit of a sugar rush should be okay, don't you think?

> *Your footprints in snow*
> *I followed, quiet, then found*
> *more behind, laughing.*

Thanks for it all,
Dave

Chapter 6
Teachers of the 1970s

"What's going on in our schools anyway? Whatever happened to the three Rs? Who does the teaching, the kids or the teacher? Does anyone discipline them now? What happened to the old learning?" So began a February 1973 feature article in the *Calgary Herald*. The *Herald* was concerned that waves of change sweeping through schools and society were making it difficult for parents to understand what was really happening in the classroom. Especially troubling was the apparent conflict between "traditional" and "progressive" education.

Cy Groves, a Calgary high-school English teacher, responded with his own *Herald* article entitled "What's Going On In Our Schools?" Groves patiently explained advantages and disadvantages of the differing philosophies, and concluded with a statement that educators (and parents) gradually accepted as the decade of the 1970s evolved: "No one knows which is the right philosophy. All one can do is to choose the educational philosophy that best suits an individual's learning style."

Groves spoke for a generation of Alberta teachers coping with societal and educational changes of the day. This chapter introduces us to innovative teachers who employed both "traditional" and "progressive" approaches in their classrooms. Here you will experience English teachers using free-form poetry, films and music, to stimulate interest in classical literature.

The 1970s also witnessed significant changes in the makeup of the province's teaching force. Alberta teachers were now drawn from more diverse ethnic and cultural backgrounds, offering role models of tolerance in their classrooms. And they were better educated than ever before, as a minimum of a university degree (first promised in 1945) became a reality for all beginning teachers seeking provincial certification.

Motivation and Mercy

by Arthur Kent

Gloria Dalton
Viscount Bennett School, Calgary

For most of my very mediocre scholastic career, I did little more than pose as a student. So it was only fitting that fate sometimes landed me in classrooms ruled by bitter, misguided disciplinarians merely masquerading as teachers. Luckily, though, as I fumbled my way through the years, I found myself looking up to some truly inspired professionals at the blackboard.

While coping with the scholastic curse of expressing my thoughts in the English language, I encountered the teacher who combined, more than any other, the two most precious virtues an instructor can possess: motivation and mercy. Gloria Dalton motivated her unruly students to think freely and get some of that thinking down on paper. And she was merciful when grading our extravagant failures—the vital first step in persuading us to try, try, and try again.

The good news is that Gloria continues to this day doing battle in the cause of greater teenage literacy. Having survived my generation of academic refusniks at Viscount Bennett, she's currently teaching at Crescent Heights. I'm sure that films and music and art are still part of her instructional repertoire. But back in the late 60s, it was nothing short of revolutionary for a high school teacher to use movie screenings to kick-start her classes in English composition. Or agree to a student's request that his next essay might mull over the guitar licks and lyrics of Jimi Hendrix. Or that instead of writing about violence, you and a couple of your classmates might just grab a super-8 camera and some old newsmagazines and produce a 3-minute animated film on the subject. And actually get graded for it.

Way back when Trudeau was a first-time PM (and a forerunner by the name of Diefenbaker was giving him hell in Parliament), Gloria's open-minded approach to education was nothing less than anarchy to some of her starchy old-school colleagues. And of course we loved her for it. Her English class was one of the few things we enjoyed as much as misbehaving. We could well have been expelled a dozen times over. For instance, we weren't above cheating on assignments. Or, while teach was out of the room, we might lock one of our pals outside the second floor window, just to see how long it'd take before he was missed. Or the day the authorities up in Edmonton lowered the drinking age to 18, and we 16-year-olds spirited our way into the Westgate to wash down our lunch with beer.

Through all of this, Gloria never gave up on us. And somewhere during those weeks and months, she placed strategically within our reading lists some of the most mind-expanding works of English literature, works we learned to take time reading, to understand and most of all to enjoy. She was one of the first teachers who told us it was all right to interpret writers and their work in different ways. We could have alternative views, contrary views—even revolutionary views. The appreciation of good storytelling wasn't a journey of straight lines. It was our own Great Escape from the strictures of old-world teaching.

By opening the doors to free thought, teachers like Gloria gave us our first inkling of what freedom truly means: the ability to rise above ignorance and prejudice; to consider the possibilities in life, rather than limit your options. These are the lessons I'm most grateful for, and for which, still today, I say thank you, Gloria. Oh, and please give the word-challenged kid in the back of the class a break for me today, OK?

Leading by Example

by Lorraine Trendiak

Joan Saxon
Brentwood Elementary School, Calgary

Grade 6—top of the heap! Woo-hoo! I just knew that 1970 was going to be the best year of school ever! The room was huge, and my teacher was beautiful. Mrs. Saxon was standing there at the front of the class ready to start. Our first assignment was to write an essay: "What I did this summer." Then Mrs. Saxon did the unheard of—she went first! I liked the idea of a teacher leading by example.

Mrs. Saxon had travelled to London, England and saw the palace where Queen Elizabeth II lived. I was so enamoured with just the idea of London. I could almost picture the gates to the palace where Mrs. Saxon was standing to watch the changing of the guards. This is the very gate, at the front of a white palace, where she met a girl called Julie Jones. I was so amazed by this adventure, that when Mrs. Saxon offered someone in the class to be a pen-pal with Julie, I almost jumped out of my skin with excitement. I volunteered right away! This was only the beginning of my memories.

Mrs. Saxon was everything that I thought a teacher should be: an educator, advisor, coach, instructor, mentor, pedagogue, confidant, helper and friend.

Through many venues, Mrs. Saxon brought my education to life. We learned to cook, studied dance, art, creative writing and music. I remember music class—the music, the piano and the singing. Fabulous!

Remember Julie Jones at the gate of the castle? Julie and I started writing to each other as pen-pals that very day. She lived in Wales, Great Britain and I lived in Calgary, Alberta, Canada. She was 12 and I was 10. Julie and I have been writing and talking on the telephone ever since. We fostered our friendship through sharing photos, talking and writing about pets, books, movies, school, parents, fashions, ideas, sports, boys, dating, marriage, homes, decorating and children. This list is long but incomplete without all of the emotion, and the heart-felt connection that is deep between two close friends. A 36-year gift—not many teachers can give that to a student!

In 1998 I wrote a letter of thanks to Mrs. Saxon and sent it to the Calgary Board of Education, asking that they forward my letter to her. It wasn't long before my phone was ringing and I was able to talk to her myself. Mrs. Saxon. Wow! We met for lunch and, as they say, the rest is history.

Joan Saxon and I are fabulous friends. We have lunch, share pictures of family, visit each other's homes, travel together, go shopping together, and have countless stories to share with each other. Although our relationship has changed, the basics are still there. She is still everything that I think a teacher should be. Now as an adult—the best part is friend!

Joan, thank you so much for the brilliant gift you gave to me by just being you!

She Obliterated the Lines of Prejudice

by Cindy Stewart

Pixie Naidoo
High Prairie Elementary School, High Prairie

It was September 2—the first day of Grade 6. I was excited. New clothes—new shoes—new books. All of this was adding to the anticipation of the new year. Along with new beginnings there was the comfort in the familiar. Same bus ride—same school—same friends.

When I got to school, I went to the Grade 6 area of the hallway. I checked the class lists posted by the doorways. I found my name on the 6-1 list. I smiled. I was a good student and this was the smart kid class. My homeroom teacher's name was Mrs. Naidoo. Hmmm, she was new. The 6-1 class lined up outside the classroom door and waited. We all knew each other. We'd been together in the same group since Grade 1. Once in a while someone from another class would move up or someone from our class would move down. It didn't matter. The school was small enough that everyone was recognizable. That made it a very big deal if there was someone new. We whispered about this Mrs. Naidoo. We lived in a small town with very familiar last names like Smith, McDermott, Stewart and Jones. Naidoo was completely foreign.

The bell rang. The classroom door opened and out into the hallway stepped a woman. She had brown skin and black hair. She wore a red and gold floor length dress that wrapped around her body. She had gold bracelets on her wrists and a red dot in the middle of her forehead. She was like nothing I'd ever seen before. I felt very uneasy.

She led us into the classroom. She wrote her name on the blackboard and told us how to pronounce it. She spoke softly. We reacted nervously.

Then Mrs. Naidoo did what she was there to do. She taught. I don't remember what projects we did or math we learned or science experiments we tried. I do remember we all went on to Grade 7. My name was on the 7–1 list.

156

What made Mrs. Naidoo a great teacher was not in the way she taught the Grade 6 curriculum; her greatness came from her ability to teach us equality and respect without ever planning a lesson on the topics. In her classroom everyone was equal. She was a wonderful role model.

During my childhood we read books like *Little Black Sambo* and studied social books that referred to Canada's Aboriginal people as "the noble savage." I knew nothing of other cultures. I lived in a small rural farming community made up of mostly second generation Eastern European settlers. Throw in a few Irish, some Scots and the native people, and that was the extent of our cultural diversity. We had only gotten television four years earlier. We were lucky if we got to see a fuzzy picture of *Hockey Night in Canada* or *Don Messers' Jubilee* . . . not much multiculturalism there.

By Grade 6 I had already been socialized to recognize the divisions among groups. In our small town, there were dividing lines between bus kids and town kids, smart kids and dumb kids, native kids and white kids. It was the general opinion of those around us that every group had a ranking and one should stay within their boundaries.

Mrs. Naidoo, just by being who she was, obliterated the lines of prejudice that had been drawn in my mind. She changed my view of the world. I revered Mrs. Naidoo so much that all notions of superiority had to be questioned and thus, erased. The "them" and "me" attitude that was so prevalent suddenly became so irrelevant.

Looking back it really was amazing. Mrs. Naidoo came to our little town in northern Alberta from halfway around the world. That had to be terrifying for her. She came to a place where not one person looked like her. No-one understood her culture. She had nowhere to buy traditional food. There was no "sari" shop in our town. Despite all of this, she did come. Thank goodness she did come.

At the end of Grade 6, Mrs. Naidoo moved from our little town. I remember helping her pack up the classroom. She gave me a poster of the Eiffel Tower. I wanted so desperately to cling to her and beg her not to leave. But, I didn't. The last bell rang and I left the classroom to catch the bus. When I looked back Mrs. Naidoo was gone.

Memories of my favourite teacher? Thirty-five years later they burn bright and clear in my mind. I see her. I smell her. I hear her. I know reflected in me are the life lessons she taught me. Anyone could have taught me math or science. Mrs. Naidoo taught me love. For that I am forever grateful.

Mr. Samborski's Moment

by Ralph Mason

Paul Samborski
Viscount Bennett School, Calgary

The aristocrats of Viscount Bennett High School were its football players. On game days, when the seventy-two members and ten teacher-coaches of the senior and junior Vikings wore their purple and gold, they strutted, as was their entitlement. Volleyball too was a fall sport, but in 1970 at Viscount Bennett it was almost totally eclipsed by football. Nevertheless, in my Grade 12 year, I switched to the sport that better suited my tall and gangly body. Twelve students signed up to play volleyball, but there was a problem. There was no coach—and without a coach there would be no team.

For two weeks we listened to the announcement over the public address system that unless a teacher volunteered to coach, the team would not operate this fall. Then, the week that the season was to begin, we were told that the first practice would be Tuesday after school!

It was the first time most of us had even seen Mr. Samborski. He looked as out of place in a gymnasium as possible. Still dressed in shirt and tie, and holding a book called *Introduction to Volleyball*, with his forefinger marking one of the earlier pages, he explained to us that he had volunteered to coach the team because he didn't want to see the team's season cancelled. There was a slight problem, though. He admitted that he wasn't much of a sports person. He'd never played volleyball. But he said he was willing to learn, and he held up the book and smiled without confidence.

"I've been reading about spiking," he said, "so we'll begin there." He glanced at his book for assurance. "From three strides back from the net, you approach the net at an angle." He proceeded to demonstrate, moving slowly in his street shoes, book in hand. "And you jump, with a two-armed swing." With that, Mr. Samborski jumped, and landed in the net. His glasses went flying. The book tumbled to the ground, and Mr. Samborski followed, hitting his knee hard on the floor.

I will finish the story, but first allow me to suggest why it mattered. I can't tell you we went on to win the city championships—we didn't, but if we'd won our last match, we would have made the play-offs. I won't tell you that I went on to play for Canada in the Olympics—I didn't. I did fall in love with the sport that fall, and played for the University of Calgary. When I became a teacher, volleyball was the sport I most loved to coach. But Mr. Samborski's Moment wasn't about the volleyball, for me.

"Well," he said, massaging his knee, "I guess I won't be helping much if I demonstrate. I'll read some more about coaching before the next practice. Perhaps you can each take a turn leading a drill, and then we'll just play for a while. Before I forget, the bus for Friday's tournament leaves the parking lot at 3:30."

We all have examples of great teachers, experts at their craft and experts in their subject areas. I suspect others hold Mr. Samborski in esteem for this, but I don't even know what subjects he taught. For me, Mr. Samborski embodied a professional courage of an even higher order. He knew that even if he tried his best, he couldn't do well what he had volunteered to do. Yet for a handful of students he didn't know, he chose to carry on, and committed to doing well enough.

Mr. Paul Samborski, you have been my embodiment of professional courage for thirty-five years. I hope your descendents and other students touched by you might read this, and know that your professionalism and dedication to students will be with me forever. You were my coach. Thank you.

The Smile of Mrs. Kostash

by Leah (Baric) McMullen

Mary Kostash
McKernan Elementary School, Edmonton

It was a cold weather classroom illuminated within by sunflowers, a Parisian sun draping shadows on an attic floor—and the smile of Mrs. Kostash.

When I look at 7-year-old children today, I marvel at their shining heads and eager hands, brains beneath bangs and quizzical frowns. I was small and my mind a clean chalkboard when I began Grade 2.

I can't recall the fall of 1970, or the next spring for that matter, because my memories of Edmonton's McKernan Elementary School are white with winter—always winter. The school was surrounded by drifts of snow, that were coaxed into recess igloos, and green, iron fencing perfect for somersaulting over. Within the school's brick embrace, I can see rows of miniature boots lining the hallway. The air was musky with the smell of melting snow, the breath of the old furnace and the scent of the phosphorescent flakes the janitor sprinkled before his broom.

Mrs. Kostash's classroom was on the main floor, the second on the right of the entrance. Well, to be honest, I can't recall the exact location of her room. But allow me this walk back into an environment I haven't actually seen for many years.

I remember being frightened of her. She was a presence. Her shoulders seemed to perfectly balance the energy of one who seldom rests. She wore dresses reminiscent of the 1950s, belted and shoulders padded, in rich maroon, indigo brocade, or the occasional, but always discreet plaid and the obligatory stockings and high-heeled pumps. A kerchief would encircle her head when she went outdoors. Unveiled, her hair was black, threaded with pearl and coiled above the nape of her elegant neck. I pause to do the arithmetic: she was 51 when I came beneath her eagle-bright gaze and straight mouth subtly outlined with ruby. My love for metaphors and similes I might owe to her. My love for the story within the artist, I owe to her as well.

160

Mrs. Kostash introduced me to a world beyond my wooden desk with its dormant inkwell. I wish I could remember everything about a day in her classroom, the names of the books she read to us, the details of the stories she urged us to write. But of course after almost thirty-one years, I can't.

I'll sit, instead, at my wooden desk for a moment, and listen to her describe a painting, *Sunflowers* by Van Gogh. Then, later, show us the portrait of the tortured artist himself, his head bandaged but his eyes open wounds, dim with hopelessness. With her I met Rembrandt: a struggling, dusty painter whose studio was a garret. She revealed to this tiny second grader the depths of his shadows and the lucidity of his light.

To this day, her descriptions and explanations form the foundation of my knowledge of art. I can't hear her voice as she taught; I only know that I still waver with the impact of her words, just as I did when they flowed into my head as I sat there at my wooden desk.

I remember music: Beethoven's *Moonlight Sonata* on a minus 28 afternoon, the sky outside our windows as night-blue as his. She told of how this nocturnal melody was created by a deaf man, futilely in love. Centuries later, in a twilight prairie classroom, the pain shared by these great artists bewitched me. To this day, I am swayed by a sunflower, a shadow, a sonata.

Then there was Tchaikovsky. As his music played, we would close our eyes and she would tell stories about the *Nutcracker Suite*. Later, we would draw what we had imagined, spending hours on the floor with our masterpieces: sketching, outlining and colouring with pencil crayons—the rich vibrant shades of vermillion, aubergine and emerald worn down and immediately re-sharpened.

I drew a harem dancer, bejewelled and gossamer-draped. She glided and whirled beneath my fingers against a backdrop of night sky as blue as Beethoven's. Drawing was never my strength, but I was amazed at how music had inspired the fantastic spirit before me. I remember Mrs. Kostash leaning over my shoulder and, from what seemed a great height, saying, "Leah, that's the best drawing you've ever done."

Her praise was hard-earned. When given, it was gold. I could have bitten down with baby teeth on the medallion she gave me at that moment. Its sheen can still illuminate the shadows of this, my adult heart.

Thank you Mrs. Kostash for such priceless currency.

Amazing Maysie
by Gord Gillies

Maysie MacDonald
Killarney Elementary School, Calgary

Class of '72. Maysie MacDonald and Gord (2nd row, far right). *Courtesy: Gord Gillies*

It was school yard legend. If you placed a hair on the palm of your hand prior to getting the strap, you would bleed. And then the school would be in big trouble!

I wasn't about to find out. Even though this was my third year in a row for corporal punishment, a hair on the palm was the last thing on my mind. I was terrified of this latest trip to the office to straighten me out. Don't get me wrong, I wasn't exactly Public Enemy #1 at Killarney Elementary School in 1971. I don't even remember why I was getting the strap again (my previous offences were throwing snowballs and kicking a volleyball). But I will admit spending a few hours on my own in the cloakroom, and I certainly knew the quickest route to the office.

There was Principal Clipperton preparing to deliver a message. About to prove his hands were just as nimble with the strap, as on the ukulele during assembly. Truth be known, I really do think it hurt him more than me. I think we both figured he'd get another chance next year.

But things were about to change. In Grade 6 I ended up in Mrs. MacDonald's class. While new to me, she had long ties to our family. Not only had she taught my brother, Scott, along the way, she'd also taught my mom! Talk about having an inside line on the parent-teacher interviews.

We clicked for a variety of reasons. Maybe it was the classroom responsibilities she gave me. Perhaps it was her encouragement for my endless doodling. She always made sure FUN was part of her daily lesson. All of a sudden class was an incredible place to be, regardless of the topic. Mrs. MacDonald inspired me to focus my extra enthusiasm in a positive way, and Grade 6 was my best year ever.

When I began to write this tribute, I phoned Killarney to get some background on Mrs. MacDonald. I didn't even know her first name. Did they remember who I was talking about? Oh yes.

Maysie MacDonald. Amazing Maysie. You know, she still lives three blocks from the school.

I had the most wonderful visit with Mrs. MacDonald the other day. We sipped a cup of tea and I mined her incredible memory. She began her teaching career in 1932 in a one-room school called Two Pine, in Bragg Creek. Yes, she rode a horse to class!

Maysie and Dolly, circa 1930s.
Courtesy: Maysie MacDonald

Playing the nosy reporter, I asked her how old she was. With a twinkle in her eyes she told me, adding, it wasn't too late to get an "F" should it appear anywhere. She remembered teaching my brother and me. Even recalls my grandma coming to meet-the-teacher night to hear how my mom was doing.

Amazing Maysie.

She still has our class picture, one of dozens in her home, featuring hundreds of smiling faces. She even happened to save a photo clipping from the *Calgary Herald* that I was a part of. There we are in class making puppets. It made the newspaper! A classroom treasure tucked away for thirty-three years. Incredibly, she remembers overhearing a conversation in the teacher's lounge half way through my sixth year at Killarney. Someone remarked: "Where's Gord Gillies? We haven't seen him in the office this year." The answer: "Maysie's got him."

Buried under one of the trees out front of Killarney Elementary School is a time capsule from the Grade 6 class of 1972. We all wrote down that Mrs. MacDonald was the best teacher EVER.

It was a three foot sapling then. Now it's grown into a towering tree, higher than the school itself. One of many little seeds planted back then. Nurtured, and watered with lots of love and encouragement.

From all of us—thank you Maysie.

The Muddy Cowboy

by Richard Craig Gorecki

Ellen Golly
F.E. Osborne Junior High School, Calgary

A hush settled over the classroom as, one by one, we became absorbed in the assignment. Our teacher, Ms. Golly, strolled up and down the aisles of her Grade 7 language arts class, radiating assurances that everyone was capable of meeting the challenge. And I vividly remember the moment I made the connection—discovered the bridge between image and word.

During earlier years of education, I had been instructed to write verse. My accumulated schoolwork included numerous examples of rhyming couplets, with subjects as varied as fishing, forest animals and family vacations. Writing poetry was not a novel pursuit when we were given the task on that snowy, mid-winter day at F.E. Osborne Junior High.

There *was* a unique dimension this time; we were to derive our poem from a photograph. In addition, we were encouraged to write in free-form—for the first time in my case, liberated from the constraints and convention of "making it rhyme." The adventure began as Ms. Golly spread out a collection of pictures on a central table, a diverse assortment gathered from magazines, brochures and newspapers.

Some of my classmates made a carefree selection while others pondered intensely, bewildered by the multitude of choices. I engaged in the process cautiously, sensing that my pick would possibly have some long-term consequence. Of course, there was the appeal of hockey players, space ships and sports cars—standard visual icons for a 12-year-old Canadian boy. But I found myself rooting past all of these, patiently searching for the one image that, more than any other, needed to be captured in word.

He might have slipped past my attention, were it not for his incredible grubbiness. For here was a man so caked in grit and grime, as to be seemingly lost in wonderment over the fact of it. The layer of wet earth even coated the telltale signs of his profession—pointy-toed boots, a wide brimmed hat and a great silver buckle. The *muddy cowboy* made the argument in a very convincing style that *he* should be my subject!

So began for me an unforgettable journey, perhaps my first real effort to explore below the surface of appearances. How did he become a rodeo cowboy in the first place? Why so much mud? Was the moment one of quiet despair or controlled celebration? Questions and possible answers began to evolve and multiply. Words began to swirl in my mind and spiral out onto the blank page, words that seemed entirely free to configure themselves and speak on their own terms.

With the sounding of the class bell, however, the mysteries of the muddy cowboy had been merely exposed, not explained. This is when Ms. Golly knelt at my side and masterfully helped me realize the greatest lesson; the discovery process is what really matters. The piece of writing itself would survive, but it was the memory of that first true poetic voyage that would provide the lasting value.

Especially when life's trials have conspired to mount an offensive, I still find tremendous freedom, solace and joy in probing an image with word. More often now, these are mental images from my own experience, ones that would otherwise remain concealed from the world. Poetry is the device by which some meaning can be revealed, extracted and shared with others, a lesson well learned under Ms. Golly's knowing-eye.

He Brought the Written Word to Life

by Maureen (Casey) Andre

Louis B. Hobson
Central Memorial High School, Calgary

My most memorable teacher was Louis B. Hobson. I attended Central Memorial High School in Calgary and had the pleasure of being in both his English 10 as well as English 30 classes in the years 1971 and 1973.

Mr. Hobson brought the written word to life for me in the form of stories and plays. To attend his class was not to be lulled to sleep—no! He would read each literary passage with gusto, incorporating drama, humour and expression in every detail. He would inspire discussion of some of life's most profound questions. Not only did he instil understanding of Shakespeare's *Hamlet*, but how it was expanded into the story and play *Rosencrantz and Guildenstern are Dead*. This developed into the philosophical discussion of the meaning of existentialism. A student dare not daydream during one of these heated discussions, as often a question was directed to one of us!

In a respectful manner, Mr. Hobson was often referred to as "Louis B." He had a commanding presence and a lively stride down the hallway. He was very much an individual, and at that impressionable age in high school, was a great role model for developing our own individualism.

Not only did he teach English, but also drama. He was so passionate about both subjects that he organized and led a group of students in 1972 to London, England for a 10-day drama tour. What a fantastic experience in London's Theatre District! Despite his overwhelming motion sickness on the plane, he emerged at our destination with his sense of humour and passion for life still intact!

I would like to thank Mr. Hobson for encouraging all creative writing, as well as instilling the ability to more fully understand the written word.

Leave Room for Miss Tillotson

by Harry Sanders

Hazel Tillotson
Calgary Hebrew School, Calgary

"May I tell a joke?" These were the first words I spoke to my future Grade 1 teacher, Hazel B. "Tillie" Tillotson, in June 1972. She had invited my kindergarten class at the Calgary Hebrew School for a Grade 1 orientation. She gave us an impressive display from her outgoing pupils: on her command, they gripped the backs of their chairs with one hand, their desks with the other, and hurdled over their chairs in unison. At the end of the session, she asked if anyone had any questions. I asked mine, and she allowed me my first public speaking audience.

In retrospect, this first exchange with Miss Tillotson—and many that followed—helped foster my present career as freelance writer and local historian. My frequent speaking engagements and media appearances began with that joke in her classroom. In my report card, she commented that I enjoyed telling stories about my hometown—what she termed my "beloved Drumheller." Outside of my family, hers was the first approval I had for telling and writing stories, which is now my life's work.

Hazel Tillotson circa 1960s.
Courtesy: Glenbow Archives PA-3249

Miss Tillotson taught me to write, and I still remember her method. Forming a lower case "e" on the board, she started with the horizontal stroke

167

and said, "You go down the hall. . ." Next came the quick circle, nearly complete, around the horizontal stroke: ". . .out the door," as though forming the circle meant opening a door. As for the gap on the right side of the letter, she added: ". . .and leave enough room for Miss Tillotson." If any student was absent that day, she would tell us to leave enough room for them instead of her. For the number five: the vertical stroke ("Go down the hall"), then the crescent at the bottom ("out the door"), and finally the horizontal stroke at the top ("and wave goodbye to Miss Tillotson").

She made creative writing notebooks for us by stapling ruled sheets of paper together, and we lined up to get them. When it was my turn, she smiled and asked, "Do you want a thick one, Harry?" I didn't know the word "thick," and replied, "No . . . I want a *fat* one."

Miss Tillotson was 78 years old when she taught me, and mine was the second last of her fifty-five classes. (The mother of one of my classmates also had Miss Tillotson as a teacher.)

In the early 1990s, when I worked at the City of Calgary Archives, an elderly man named Clifford Jones came to see construction photographs of the Glenmore Dam, a Depression relief project on which he had worked. For no apparent reason, Mr. Jones showed me a letter he had carried in his wallet for years. It was from his Grade 1 teacher, H.B. Tillotson. We had both been her students, fifty years apart. In another coincidence, the woman who replaced me at the City Archives was Lisa Tillotson, Hazel's great niece.

Miss Tillotson had a wonderful smile that revealed her affection for the students and her genuine love for her work. It's been thirty years since I last saw her, but I think of Miss Tillotson often, and I expect I always will.

She Made Us Feel Very Special

by Jacqueline (Campeau) Hoare

Margaret Perry
Kensington Road Elementary School, Calgary

Grade 4 was a very turbulent year for me and my family. We had moved from a small town in central Alberta to the City of Calgary at the end of the summer of 1972. I remember feeling very anxious about being in the big city, and starting in a new school after only knowing small-town life. Our whole world had been turned upside-down. We had to leave our home and friends behind and the life we knew, to come to a world of busy streets, traffic lights and shopping malls.

Apprehensive and unsure, I remember starting my first day of school at Kensington Road Elementary. Mrs. Perry was my teacher. Being a new kid, she immediately made me feel comfortable in her classroom; she was an amazing teacher. Mrs. Perry had a gift with children. She made each and everyone of us feel very special. I remember she and her husband had the whole class over to their home in Parkdale for a backyard picnic. What a privilege to have been invited to their home. I felt so very special when Mr. and Mrs. Perry took several of us from her class to see the *Swan Lake* ballet at the Jubilee Auditorium on their own time and expense. I had never had been to anything like it. It was magical. That memory of feeling so special that night has always stayed with me.

Mrs. Perry taught me to appreciate music. She used to play the harpsichord in class and sing old songs; I still remember *Red River Valley*. Mrs. Perry was so patient preparing her fourth grade class for the school's Christmas concert. We played a fabulous hand bells rendition of *Jingle Bell Rock*. And our class trip to the legislative buildings on the school bus was a highlight. I experienced so much in that year. I even saved my report on Africa that we did in social studies.

During parent teacher interviews, Mrs. Perry told my mom "Not to break her spirit." I didn't really know what that meant at the time. I didn't know that I had a spirit—that was news to me. As I grew older I always remembered the kindness of Mrs. Perry and what a gift she was to me in my life journey. She nurtured and tended to my spirit. Whenever life was difficult, I remembered her words "Don't break her spirit." I held on tight to keep my spirit intact.

Today, I am a Hospice Chaplain, tending to the spirits of the dying. I would like to thank Mrs. Perry for tending to my spirit, for instilling passion in me for learning and for the love of music, and for sharing the gift of her spirit with me to share with others.

She Resonates in My Teaching

by Ray Suchow

Rae Tompkins
Athlone Elementary School, Edmonton

I cried when I found out my Grade 1 teacher had died. That I was in my early thirties at the time, a father, husband and teacher as well didn't matter. For that moment, as I read the obituary, and for many melancholy hours afterward, I recalled and reflected on the memories that came surging back across a span of twenty-five years.

Mrs. Rae Tompkins was born to be a Grade 1 teacher. In the growing bustle of northwest Edmonton in the early 1970s, when 137th Avenue was the absolute edge of town and the communities of Athlone, Kensington and Wellington, rang with the sounds of children who could play outside all day and didn't need to come inside until they were hungry, or it was dark—or both—she displayed that unique and critical blend of God-given skills that to this day still convince me that Grade 1 teachers are one of the most crucial elements in any educational system.

She was in her mid-forties at the time, and had a grandmother-like, matronly quality that let children know they could hug her while at the same time garnering their respect with just a glance. She had patience, the style of which I'd never seen before (being only in Grade 1). I would later understand it as unflappable. However, when she combined that patience with a measured, even tone that held your attention, she had us in the palm of her hand—and we were happy to be there.

She engaged us in many ways, some of which were decades ahead of their time. She brought a radio into the classroom for our music lessons. We listened in awe to a live radio voice in our classroom and the music he played. Afterwards, she would repeat parts of the songs on an old upright piano (which she wheeled herself into the classroom every time, though it dwarfed her) and we would sing along.

Overall, perhaps the most important thing she taught me was respect for others. As I grew, and particularly as I began my career and sought to find my own teaching style, of all the teachers I looked back on for inspiration she repeatedly came to mind as that crucial element resonated in her teaching. My classmates and I felt special in her class, and when she would initiate activities, such as asking the three early readers in her class to stand and read a passage to the rest of the class in order to demonstrate how the intonation and pacing should sound, we were happy to do so because we felt as if we were a respected part of a family. My lifelong love of reading and learning came from seeing and participating in such formative processes.

Thankfully, my final memories of her are happy ones. When I began junior high, I often returned to visit. However, as high school transitioned into university and the pace of life continued to accelerate, I wondered how she was doing. I meant to go back and tell her that I had set my heart on becoming a teacher and that she was the primary inspiration for that monumental choice, but things continued to delay that day.

Mercifully, the day did come. My weekend job in the food industry seldom had me out of the kitchen, but one of the few days it did coincided with her deciding to have dinner there. Eagerly, and a little shyly, after all she would always be my Grade 1 teacher and I still felt like a six-year-old, I introduced myself as it had been six years since I'd last seen her. I quickly recounted my progress to date and of my decision to become a teacher. Most importantly, I was able to tell her that she was the one. She had inspired me, and continued to do so as my training progressed. I was able to thank her for all she had done. Her congratulations on my choice, her smile, and her quiet thanks sent my heart soaring. All too quickly, I had to say goodbye and return to my duties. It was the last time I saw her alive.

Much later, as my years of teaching turned into a decade and beyond, I realized how rare it is for students to come back and visit their teachers. Life and work, studies and friends, all take their measure from any given week. I am so grateful that I received the final chance to say thank you.

I will never forget Rae Tompkins. As she lives on in my heart and in my mind, she will never truly die. And, as she resonates in my teaching (as parts of all our teachers do, especially the great ones) neither will the lessons she began so many years ago.

He Enriched My Life

by Lynette Klemmensen

Gary Reagan
Standard School, Standard

It was somewhere between obsessing about David Cassidy and a civil service career that I became totally aware of how integral Gary Reagan has been to my happiness. The word that most aptly describes his impact on my life: *enrichment*, and his influence certainly enriched my life both personally and professionally.

Just as important as his instruction about the mechanics of the English language, so was his ability to teach the mechanics of lifelong learning. Gary Reagan's remarkable character qualities were catalytic to sustained and meaningful learning. He incited enthusiasm about learning. He facilitated learning at different levels of awareness. He enabled spontaneity in learning—the ability to see the big picture of life, not just small fragmented snapshots. This is the essence of Gary Reagan, the teacher: just as important as the content learned, is the context in which it is taught.

My first contact with Gary Reagan was in the early 1970s. Fresh out of university, he came to Standard to teach high school English.

He has always reminded me of the type of person one would be if you melded Cary Grant and the "Professor" from *Gilligan's Island* into one. Like Cary Grant, he was poised and unflappable. He possessed a very calming and kind grace. Unfailingly, he always knew the appropriate action for the given situation. Like the Professor, he was a "generalist", extremely knowledgeable, particularly about the mechanics of the English communicative process. Just as the Professor could synthesize his knowledge about kinetics and Gilligan's muscles into functional energy, Gary Reagan could also synthesize his knowledge of "man against man", "man against the environment", and "man against himself" into real-life situations. And, as the Professor's resourcefulness was pivotal to the enhancement of the quality of life for the seven cast-a-ways, so was Gary Reagan's resourcefulness critical to enthusiastic, meaningful, and spontaneous learning.

Learning environments in the early 1970s, especially in a small rural community, were much like Gilligan's Island; limited and very low-tech. Teaching aids were simple: blackboard, chalk, and a red pen for marking. For a student, a Hilroy scribbler and disposable Bic pen were really all that was required. Visual sensory stimulation was limited to a portrait of the Queen and chocolate-bar ads, cleverly disguised as maps. A student relied on the *World Book Encyclopaedia* for research data, not the Internet. With such an unencumbered, low-tech lifestyle, a teacher's role and teaching strategies were much different than today.

Rather than perceiving his role as teacher as the omnipotent presence in the classroom, it was clearly evident that Gary Reagan viewed his function more as the person who facilitated learning. His resourcefulness and innovation were instrumental in viewing the world from new angles. Lessons were not limited to the blackboard and texts. Awareness at a deeper level than the written word resulted in formulating and applying opinions. Learning was interactive. His calming and respectful demeanour cocooned a safe, inviting, and comfortable learning environment. He was thorough and prepared. Gary Reagan's lessons were masterfully organized and deliberate. There was a confidence and credibility in his teaching.

Throughout my life, the light bulb above my head has often illuminated brightly, and I know it was Gary Reagan manning the switch. He taught how to learn, not just what to learn. His character qualities served as a benchmark, defining the requirements for successful and ethical careers. He instilled the value of challenging oneself. Perhaps more significantly, his influence extends to all the lives that his former students have touched. I certainly know the magnitude and the value of his multiplier effect.

The Joy She Had in Teaching

by Suzanne (Morrissette) Karsten

Claire Harris
St. Gregory Junior High and Bishop Carroll High School, Calgary

In the early 1970s, I was a student attending St. Gregory Junior High School in Calgary. I was one of thirty-three "unenergized" Grade 9 students that year—with a touch of attitude and a ton of cynicism. From a teacher's vantage point, our faces may have appeared to be saying: "Go ahead; I dare you to try and teach us anything."

Nothing could have prepared us for the English teacher we were gifted with that year. She emulated love and concern with a motherly-calm attitude and style. This was *not* a woman who required validation by the likes of us! As I write the vignettes about Miss Harris, I begin to see similarities to the teacher icon: actor Sidney Poitier in *To Sir with Love*.

The first classroom session was spent familiarizing ourselves and sharing stories back and forth. The details she received from us that day were the very ones that parents couldn't pry out with force. Miss Harris made a choice to invite us into her world, and we willingly accepted hook, line and sinker. "Spellbinding" and "magical" are the words I'll use in an attempt to describe this teacher's qualities.

To express the joy she had in teaching her language arts subject; her feet, her hands and her eyes danced around the room. She was intent on drawing in even the furthest student in the room. Once her mission was accomplished, and her point made, her trademark would be a quick, "Okay?" and a giggle, or a chuckle, and constant grinning too!

Her program was so attractive because she welcomed our input and her sheer delight that followed a job well-done. I recall some of the projects and assignments she required of us and the energy we put into them; no doubt a sign that we were aiming to please her. She delivered her classroom sessions like a main course, and has us yearning for more (please). Thirty-five years have passed but her charm remains fresh in my mind.

The freedom to express thoughts, prose and poetry without boundaries and limitations was the very thing we needed, and we thrived on it. This was perfect preparation for the challenges we would meet at the new high school. The first model school project in Canada was opening its doors to us, and, to our surprise, Miss Harris was also moving there. Bishop Carroll High School was geared towards teaching through unit packs and self-direction, rather than a classroom environment. So, although Miss Harris would not be as visible to us, it was reassuring that she was grading our efforts and seeing us through to our diploma.

I have found that the language arts have become a great factor in my lifestyle and my creative ventures. I'm a romantic at heart and my art-work is fuelled by the stimulant of words. I am an avid reader and am able to discuss and share books with a group of women in my community. My three children have never been denied volumes of material to enjoy. To this day I cannot part with so many of the dearly loved and cherished stories we had shared night after night.

Claire Harris has left her impression on me, for the skills and love of the written word she brought to all of us at St. Gregory. The bounty of this gift keeps surfacing as my life evolves, and therefore I know that I've received quite a treasure in this Jamaican form. In admiration of one special lady, I am sending this wordy bouquet ensuring that not another day passes without my gratitude being sent her way. Thanks so very much Miss Harris.

Dreaming Dinosaurs

by Darren Tanke

Ted Downard
Dr. E.P. Scarlett High School, Calgary

The positive influences of one's childhood teachers are not often appreciated until later in life. While I had several such teachers during my youth, a memorable one in particular stands out. He was Mr. Ted Downard, my high-school art teacher at Dr. E.P. Scarlett High School in Calgary during 1976–1979. At that time I was developing a deep passion for, of all things, dinosaurs, which put me at a disadvantage with my classmates who had bigger career dreams and aspirations.

Darren Tanke, living his dream.
Courtesy: Darren Tanke

Dinosaurs?! Get a life! But as we shall see, I ended up pursuing my dream. At that time, my whole life seemed to revolve around dinosaurs, which then did not have anywhere near the popularity or cultural acceptance they have now. When it came to art class, while others made clay pinch pots, I became interested in making clay horned dinosaur skulls and skeletons. Due to my classmates' negativity towards dinosaurs, I rather timidly approached Mr. Downard with my idea, which he immediately endorsed and encouraged.

With no real experience in anatomy, soon I had completed the first, of a number, of clay dinosaur skulls and, later on, whole skeletons. Hundreds of delicate little clay bones had to be patiently hand-built and quickly began to fill the classroom. Mr. Downard frowned on having to carefully load each and every one into the kiln, so I was given the job of loading and unloading the kiln, a duty I did for several years for all the art students. Also at this time, I was working on a massive series of dinosaur reports as part of a Special Projects 30 class, about 300 pages upon completion. All of this activity taught me many things dinosaurian and made me feel really confident about my chosen career in palaeontology.

So how was Mr. Downard so influential? Immediately after graduating from high school, I joined the palaeontology department at the Provincial Museum in Edmonton, first as a volunteer helping collect dinosaur fossils, then as a paid employee collecting my beloved horned dinosaur bones and preparing them for scientific research and display. This field and laboratory work required much patience and manual dexterity learned and honed in my high school art classes. Reconstructing the real dinosaur bones required hand-building, carving and artistic capability.

Soon I was transferred down to Drumheller to help build exhibits for the Tyrrell Museum of Palaeontology which opened in 1985. Eventually I became a technical assistant to Dr. Philip Currie, Canada's premier dinosaur researcher at Tyrrell, and after hours began conducting my own research. Now, over twenty-five years later, I am still there, finding, collecting, preparing and reconstructing fossils; interacting with palaeontologists worldwide; publishing papers on my own and with others; and doing research on the horned dinosaurs I came to love in school. And I have had fun doing it all! While I have lost track of most of my high school friends, my attendance at two high school reunions suggests I was the only one that actually pursued his dinosaur dream.

Every now and then, while reconstructing the giant skull of some prehistoric creature, I gratefully think of Mr. Downard and thank him for actively supporting my early interest in dinosaurs.

Miss O
by J.A. McDougall

Margaret Ortman
St. Boniface, Calgary

Miss Ortman never tolerated unruly behaviour; her sharp tongue could be counted on to correct those who wasted time. This was especially clear to students as, one day, a distracted boy was sent down the street during class. "Get over to the Hurdy Gurdy and pick me up a burger and fries," she said. "You're not listening to anything in here anyways." Shoving a five-dollar bill into his sweaty hand, she clamped her purse shut.

Class of 1978–79. (Jennifer McDougall top row, far left. Miss O far right.) *Courtesy: J.A. McDougall*

Younger students were terrified of our unsmiling teacher; however, we took pride in surviving her class. I marvelled at the respect she garnered in spite of her approach. Some kids called her "mean," but most understood, somehow, that there was more to Miss O than she revealed between nine and three. One afternoon in January, I was granted a peek.

"Today we will create a bar chart. Please answer the following question in your heads." Miss O tapped her temple with a red fingernail. She drew a yellow line down one side and another across the bottom of the green chalkboard. After numbering each axis, 1 to 8 and 1 to 30, she turned to us. "The question is: how many people live in your house?"

"Do we include pets?" The blond girl beside me always had something to add. Miss O's answer came fast: "I said 'people'!" No one dared speak up again.

"Raise your hand if there are two people in your house." No one moved. "Raise your hand if there are three people in your house." The arms of two children shot up. She drew a rectangle indicating two three-person households.

179

Facing us she said, "Four? Five?" Raising my hand tentatively, I shrugged. I was itching to ask for clarification, but afraid to make her angry. My special circumstance excited me so much I could burst.

"Six?" I raised my hand again. Hands on hips, she spoke. "You, missy. How many houses do you have?" I blushed, "My mom is going to have a baby and. . ." Miss O cut me off with the curve of her finger. I stood, and was directed behind the chalkboard. The invitation was both worrisome and exciting. Well-behaved students didn't generate much attention from Miss O. In private she whispered, "How many in your house?" "It depends . . ." She shook her head. "Five, I guess." I didn't want our rendezvous to end. She winked, "Good girl. When baby comes, there'll be six, right? When is mommy due?" Miss O offered a mint from her skirt pocket, and then popped one into her mouth. She let me tell her about the crib, the clothes and the diapers. I saw her smile.

In that moment, I saw the stern presentation as a means to an end, a method of capturing our attention; maintaining order. Beneath the surface, Miss O was a compassionate woman who cared about students. More importantly, she delivered complete lessons, whose subjects she had mastered.

From Miss O we received terse instruction and witty responses rather than the soft words and gentle accommodation we had come to expect in elementary school. She was the first teacher to challenge us to respect her in spite of her approach. After Miss O, I was able to find something to respect in every teacher who followed.

I learned that it was not necessary to appease people to be respected. The reasons I appreciated my fifth-grade teacher had nothing to do with kindness or her personal qualities. After all, none of us really knew her personally. Her example showed me I could accomplish things in unwelcoming environments, and that some tasks require firm leadership.

Now I am a mother, and there are days I revisit past lessons for guidance. When I feel as though I am fumbling through the parenting maze, I recall Miss O. I am inspired by her ability to balance firm boundaries and high expectations with unwavering dedication and enormous patience grounded in love for her charges.

He Made Social Studies Come to Life

by Joyce Uhrbach

Cyril Richards
Matthew Halton High School, Pincher Creek

A flood of memories washed over me as I perused the Alberta Centennial invitation carefully stuffed in my mailbox at school. My most memorable teacher—that was an easy assignment—for one quickly popped into mind. I recall from an early age, perhaps four-years old, the "big kids" nattering about "Sly Cy", the school principal. Rumour had it that he had eyes in the back of his head and, heaven forbid, if you ever got sent to the "sweat box", his office. To a youngster in the '50s this talk held somewhat of a morbid fascination, so I watched; I watched Mr. Richards carefully.

"Big C" lived in the east end of town, a fair hike to his high school, and so did I. I could see him stoke the coal and wood stove on the winter mornings and then, a little while later, walk past my window burdened down with his briefcase and lunch. Then, about 5:30 p.m., he'd return, briefcase and all. Day after day, in rainstorm, blizzard or howling wind, he made the trek . . . and I watched. At night, I could see his living-room lamp brought to the kitchen table and spread before him were mounds of social studies papers to be marked. I'm not sure when the light went out for I was sent to bed.

And the "big kids" (a.k.a. my oldest sister and her chums) talked as they cranked up Elvis Presley and ate the latest fad (Miracle Whip sandwiches) and I listened. They chatted about the school dances and Mr. Richards' "no shenanigans" rules. They talked about the leather strap and chewing gum all in the same breath, about his zero tolerance of skipping and smoking, and about the dreaded detention room. They shared the secret about listening for the squeak of his leather shoes coming down the hallway—the early warning signal for all involved in covert classroom behaviour. Yet I wondered.

I wondered as I watched him at the local hockey rink, stick handling with finesse as he coached his young NHL hopefuls, or at the community baseball diamond pitching balls and signalling plays to his minor leaguers, or the summers he waved goodbye to his family as he headed north to Edmonton to mark departmentals. How could one devote so much time to children? The word *passion* came to mind.

Then that fearful day arrived in 1970. It was my turn to be in his class. My older sister had prepped me well for this day and I fretted. But fear soon dissipated for in "C.P.R.'s" class there was control, high expectations, mutual respect between teacher and learner—and, oh, how he could teach social studies. The subject came to life for, you see, Mr. Richards had lived history—the Great Wars, the Depression, the atomic bomb, the lunar landing. He'd lived those events. Best of all, sprinkled throughout the lessons were humour and stories. Stories about his early teaching days in the Crowsnest Pass when goats were herded into the school or boys skated on the polished hardwood floors with hobnail boots. Or in Breton, Alberta when young black children walked to his country school in bare feet carrying fried jackrabbit in their lunch pails. Or in Pincher Creek where the high school was above the town's jail cells and the excitement this generated on certain mornings! I learned my stuff that year not because I had to, but because I wanted to.

Graduation day soon arrived at my old alma mater. My decision on life's ambition had been sealed. I desired to become a teacher like Mr. Richards—to make a difference in a child's life, like he had done in mine and so many before me. And so, it came to pass that four years later, Mr. Richards and myself shared a "stage" together. He was putting down the chalk after forty-three years of dedicated teaching, and I was picking it up for the first time. "To make a difference. . ." Thanks, Dad.

Quiet, Stable, and Reassuring

by Wayne Hunt

Paul Shaw
St. Matthew Junior High School, Calgary

Mr. Shaw was bland . . . very bland. To us he seemed to wear the same brown suit everyday. We were all waiting for the day he would go wild and wear a grey suit. He was not the type who would jump around at pep rallies or make a lot of announcements on the public address system. He was always just there; quiet, but stable and reassuring. To us young adults in junior high on the precipice of drugs, relationships and the world, his style was just what we needed.

Mr. Shaw especially supported the children from one-parent families, of which I was one. Maybe he could see that some of us were struggling, and that he could fill this need. The extra attention was subtle and not overly expressive, that was not his way.

After I had set a record in the 440 yard run, Mr. Shaw mentioned to me, "I have never seen you move that fast in the hallways." Even though I was young, I knew there was a compliment in there somewhere. It wasn't much, but it was attention.

When I remember my school days the most salient ones are the very good days and bad days. In Grade 7, getting the strap caused a bag of mixed emotions. To the other children this was a badge of honour, and they called you words like "cool" and "far out". The other emotions included pain. The teacher who delivered the strap had been on a pedestal, but he fell a long way down. I was strapped for throwing a paper airplane in class (it must have been the straw that broke the camel's back; they wouldn't strap you for lofting a plane, would they?) In the next class, Mr. Shaw took me aside and said, "You would not make a good poker player, your emotions are all over your face." Of course, I was too embarrassed to tell him why, but I am sure he soon determined the reason. His concern got me through that day; it wasn't one of my better ones.

In the middle of February the weather turned unbearably cold, and Mr. Shaw stopped coming to school. Most of the students in their absorbed ways did not notice, but the unofficial one-parent club noticed. We knew that something was missing.

In the spring Mr. Shaw came back, but something was different. His appearance had changed and he had to hold up one side of his mouth when he spoke. He also walked with a limp now, and it was noticeable. We did not know what happened, but we knew he was not the same. In junior high we had never heard of words like "stroke", so we spoke to him in the same cheerful manner we always had. Though he had to hold up his mouth to speak to us, I believe that we helped him. Even though his world had turned upside down, we remained constant.

The school year was coming to an end and I noticed Mr. Shaw walking down the hall between class changes. His limp was still noticeable. He stopped and leaned against the lockers for a moment with his head looking down. He did not see me but I stood transfixed behind him in the hallway. The other students didn't seem to notice him and went to their classes. The hallway was now clear of everybody except for me and Mr. Shaw. A pin could be heard dropping in the hallway, the only sound being the teachers starting their lessons. He stood there for what seemed like a long time, but it was probably only a few minutes. I could not move. I wanted to take him by the arm and help him back to his office, but the student–vice-principal barrier was too much to overcome. Finally Mr. Shaw lifted his head and continued walking to his office, and I went to my class.

As with the other students, I became absorbed in track and field, and the excitement of moving on to senior high school. I cannot remember saying goodbye to Mr. Shaw, so I would like to say it now. Just as you helped us, I will help students who are struggling. Good-bye Mr. Shaw and thank you.

Chapter 7
Teachers of the 1980s

The 1980s served as transition years for Alberta schools and their teachers. Conservative pressures throughout North American society forced education systems to rein in many of the more radical changes of the free-wheeling 1960s and '70s, and to re-introduce such traditional approaches as core curriculum and standardized examinations. Yet Alberta teachers maintained—and often improved on—various innovative approaches that strengthened curriculum and enhanced student learning.

This chapter spotlights a number of teachers whose classrooms sparkled with creative projects, hands-on-learning, and inspired students. And teachers who provided valuable role models for students experiencing difficult times as they moved through the often angst-ridden years of childhood, puberty and teenage life.

Here you can read of the inspirational work of teachers like David Foster, Janet Groeneweg. Lily Pentek, Alvina First Rider, Cathy Gauthier, Andrew Luyken, Glynn Searl, Denis Routhier, Max Foran and Kally Krylly—ten teachers representative of the province's educators during this decade.

A Man Ahead of His Time

by Corinne (Egger) Cookshaw

David Foster
Westgate Elementary School, Calgary

He was not everyone's favourite teacher. But, for me, he opened up a whole new world of learning, exploring and believing in myself.

I was not a conventional student. I managed just fine. My marks were alright, but mostly my teachers and I just did not understand each other. In spite of this, I liked school. I liked to learn and each year brought new and exciting things.

1980: Westgate School in Calgary. I had been looking forward to Grade 5 until I discovered, to my horror, who my teacher would be. Mr. Foster was strict, with a loud voice and an emphatic temper. Now I was stuck with him for the whole year—I actually went home and cried!

I had grossly misjudged him; just like I was an unconventional student, he was an unconventional teacher. My independent spirit soared as I discovered the ways in which he deviated from the structured approach to education that I had experienced so far. First we moved our desks outside of the unimaginative arrangement of perfect rows. By allowing us to form groupings of our choosing, Mr. Foster showed us that he trusted us. For the first time in my young life I was not just being shuffled along with the rest of the crowd as someone else's responsibility. I hardly recognized this at the time, but I certainly enjoyed this departure from the structure that I had found so confining.

He made learning fun. We watched films; we sang along while he played on the guitar—songs that were familiar to us and songs that he taught us from his native New Zealand.

Every year there were two big creative projects in Mr. Foster's class. These were hands-on projects that the Grade 5 students came to look forward to. The first of these projects was an illustrated story. He did not ask us to just sit down and write a story. Instead, we started a long term story project in which we would devote time each week to developing the story, the characters, the structure. And then we would illustrate our stories; not just draw a picture, but create a series of pictures with a common theme that would add impact to the story that we had written. When the stories were done, we made two copies, one for ourselves and one for the school library where they we available for everyone to read. We had created not just an exercise in writing or expression— but a book. We were no longer just kids who were not old enough to do anything meaningful. Now we could make something from start to finish, something that was an expression of ourselves as we pulled the parts together into a cohesive whole. It was empowering.

The other project was the production of a film. Instead of saying, "Now this is what we are going to do," Mr. Foster said, "What would you like to do?" And we brainstormed and we discussed and we reasoned about what would be practical and he helped us to understand in a small way what we could do with just a movie camera and our imaginations.

None of this seems quite so special today in the enlightened age of education that we are currently in. Teachers and teaching organizations now recognize the value of using innovative methods to help students learn, but Mr. Foster was ahead of his time. He may not have helped me conform—which might have helped me get through the rest of my schooling without confrontations with my teachers—but he helped me build a stronger self-identity, which enabled me to learn from all my teachers that followed, allowed me to thrive in university where suddenly you are the *only* one responsible for yourself, and empowered me to proceed through my life with confidence and to seek learning, not only from books, but also from experience.

Each Day Had a Cause for Celebration

by Alicia Reimer

Janet (Groeneweg) Greenway
Sunnyside Elementary School, near Lethbridge

Dear Teacher,

I so clearly remember walking into my Grade 1 classroom and choosing my desk at the front, left corner. You had on a green pantsuit that first day to help us remember your name. When you announced this, we all giggled. I knew already that I loved you, not as my mother, but for a little while each day, in place of her.

I remember the first word you taught us to print: r-e-d. You perfectly printed the letters on the chalkboard and I tried my very best to copy them exactly. Although I have some memories of the content you taught, the majority of my memories are centred on you, and the many ways you encouraged us to enjoy life.

When the weather permitted, you would take us outside for long walks around the playground. I remember how you taught us that we could eat the tiny bread and butter plants that grew around the edges of the school yard, and how you really had me believing that they tasted like bread and butter! You were also willing to share laughter with us on our level. I remember how you would sometimes rest your feet on your desk and then laugh when we reminded you that you never let us put our feet on our desks.

You saw to it that each day had a cause for celebration. It thrilled me when you would come around to each desk at lunchtime and snoop through our plastic lunchboxes exclaiming over the wonderful food our mothers had packed. We even celebrated the cold, winter weather; we had to bundle up and go outside for fresh air just until our cheeks turned rosy (which I never felt was quite fair, since my best friend had permanently red cheeks!). During the year's holidays, you made a big deal out of the little things, like coming around to our desks on Valentine's Day with one or two cinnamon hearts, just for a little break now and again.

I realize now that you knew that, as a Grade 1 student, I needed to be noticed. I loved it when you would read to us on the carpet at the back of the room. What made it that much better was when you noticed that I loved to read and passed the book to me, asking me to read to the whole class—I felt so important!

Your influence shaped my life. I am now a teacher, and I do my best to remember what you taught me, not about printing or reading, which I know my own students may forget in the years to come, but about life. I try to laugh with my students, celebrate life with my students, and notice my students. Thank you for teaching me these things.

Sincerely,
A Pupil

Mama Lily

by Susanna Pankiw

Lily Pentek
F.G. Miller School, Elk Point

A corner in her home is filled with Golden Globes of a different kind. These pictorial medals are a small representation of the many lives she has touched along her teaching journey, mine are among them.

The first time I met Mama Lily, a short, feisty Italian, I was apprehensive about my placement in her Grade 9 English class in 1983. I even considered trying to transfer over to the other class, which I knew wasn't going to happen. So, initially, trudging off to the course everyday wasn't an uplifting experience. Mrs. Lily Pentek was very disciplined, gave homework frequently and had high expectations for her students (something that I had not been accustomed to).

Then came those dreaded weekly journals. Ugh! At first I completed them because they were required, then something extraordinary happened! I began to feel comfortable with this lady, which was something that I had never felt with any other teacher in my life. I was able to open up to her and communicate on a completely different level through my journals. I felt like I could truly trust this person. I would even write to her about things that I felt I could not tell my mother. Lily was in no way judgmental or a preacher. She briefly, but tactfully, replied to my concerns in such a way that I was left with time for inner reflections. This, I think, was intentional.

Through these journals she became a source of encouragement. My secret love of poetry flourished and so did the beginnings of my poetry writing.

Then came Grade 10, which left me feeling lost and lonely. In a time where my life was beginning to change I was also suffering from withdrawal symptoms; I had been assigned to a different teacher for this year. I had begun to rely on my weekly, personal discussions with Mrs. Pentek and began to appreciate her moderate dose of solemn and wise words.

After this long void, the rest of my high-school English days were greeted with the ultimate antidote—Mrs. Pentek. Over these next two years I felt that we had become close and that I had gained a fundamental piece of my life's pie. Mrs. Pentek became my friend and confidant and eventually earned the highest honour (in my books) to be called Mama. She was, indeed, like having a second mother.

I had always embraced this person as my "special" secret. We continued to stay in contact after I left school and I was content to keep this information undisclosed. It wasn't until years later that I visited her at her home that I realized my secret was shared with many other students. The pictures of previous students' children that lined her walls were the result of her innate ability to connect to, understand and make each one of us feel unique.

Mama Lily was (and still is) a positive and influential person in my life. She is the picture of dedication, concern and kindness that can't easily be replicated or replaced. I can't imagine my life without her. She is one of the reasons for my continued perseverance in the writing field, for without her initial and continual words of encouragement I would not have had the ability to take the first steps. In retrospect, she may have been one of the reasons I became a teacher. She is the ultimate source of inspiration and I can only hope that when I end my teaching career that my students remember me fondly like I remember Mama Lily. This is the best award anyone could ask for.

She Told Me I Would Be a Future Leader

by Sandra Crazy Bull

Alvina First Rider
Kainai High School, Cardston

In Grade 8, inside a little portable used as a classroom, on a Blood Indian Reserve called Kainai, my teacher, Mrs. Alvina First Rider, taught me how to be respectful.

The recent death of my mother, coupled with the fact that back then most of our teachers gave us little or no room to be proud of ourselves as First Nations' people, made me a most difficult young 13-year-old. My daily routine of disruptive outbursts included turning the music to its highest volume, scribbling over her notes on the blackboard and leaving while she was teaching. My teacher responded with patience and kindness; she seemed to never be affected by bad behaviour and would continue as though it never happened; she displayed peaceful, well-balanced attributes which turned out to be a blessing to me. Mrs. First Rider told me back then, in 1984, that I would be a future leader to which I responded, "Whatever." She gave me a little piece of obsidian which I keep in a beaded leather bag around my neck right next to my heart.

One day as I was teaching my class at the Glenbow Museum in the Nitsitapiisinni: Our Way of Life Gallery, Mrs. First Rider strolled through. She had a big smile on her face as she saw me leading the class. I had come full circle and was the teacher now. When I had a minute I went to speak to her and we hugged and laughed and she said, "I always knew you were going to make it!" "You haven't seen a bad girl until you've had *me* in your class!" I think she meant I was no match to her as a "bad girl".

As an educator, I often reflect on the serene nature of my teacher Mrs. First Rider—this offers a breath of fresh air and renewed thoughts of showing kindness and respect to my students.

She Challenged Me

by Meisha Hunter

Cathy Gauthier
St. Bonaventure Junior High School, Calgary

Recently, I was speaking with a colleague about teachers who made a difference in our lives. I spoke about my Grade 8 English teacher, Mrs. Cathy Gauthier, and how she challenged me, and believed in me when I didn't believe in myself.

When I was growing up in Calgary, I used to be extremely shy. Short, nervous, extremely fearful, always looking at my watch or my feet, unable to make small talk or look others in the eye, often being beaten up at school, spat on, verbally insulted. Since my mom worked the night shift, I would often walk home for lunch, cry, eat, and grudgingly go back. I had no self-confidence to speak of—no friends. I remember saving up my babysitting money once to buy a SunIce jacket that all the popular girls wore, hoping it would help me to fit in. Needless to say, there were lots of problems going on at home which I didn't know how to cope with. I was like a hollow shell of a person, numb, just trying to survive day to day.

I still remember sitting in Mrs. Gauthier's classroom. I remember her long skirts, her blonde bobbed hair, and her winning smile. She insisted that I take a lead role in the school Christmas play. I'll probably never forget the name of the character—Mrs. Cavendish—a miserly old woman (like a female Scrooge) who intended to sell a building that was leased to an orphanage, putting all the children on the street. I had never acted, didn't know how to speak above a whisper. After trying to get myself out of it, I decided to accept my fate. Mrs. Gauthier knew the one thing I needed most was to take a risk and try something different: put my "self" aside for a while, try being in the spotlight. I learned how to stand and walk with confidence, speak loudly and convincingly, converse (however staged) with other people, laugh at my mistakes, and feel part of a group.

After that play, I signed up for public speaking and debate teams, joined a support group for kids, read at St. Bonaventure Church, started to develop friends of my own. Twenty years later, you probably wouldn't recognize me if you had known me from my St. Bonaventure days. I work as an architectural historian for the Landmarks Preservation Commission in New York, helping to preserve and regulate changes to designated landmarks throughout the city. I make presentations in front of a board every week as part of my job, and speak intermittently at professional conferences and meetings. I look people in the eye, I speak (much of the time) with confidence and integrity, I believe in myself.

I am so grateful for the opportunity to submit this brief letter of praise for Mrs. Gauthier. I could have resigned my memory of her to a brief mention in infrequent conversations about great teachers. I can't tell you how many times I have mentioned Mrs. Gauthier to family and friends over the years and how much she meant to me. God knows why I never thought to try to tell her personally, until now. Her enthusiasm, generosity of spirit, dedication, concern about my welfare, and her willingness to go above and beyond her primary responsibilities, made her stand out as a character-defining person for me.

He Helped Break the Cycle

by Judy Dickson

Andrew Luyken
St. Thomas More School, Fairview

Moving up from elementary to junior high at St. Thomas More School in Fairview was not a big deal. You didn't change schools and you didn't get new faces wandering through the halls. The only difference from Grade 6 to 7 was a locker upstairs and a lot more homework.

Andrew Luyken. *Courtesy: St. Thomas More School*

When I entered Grade 7, in 1985, the most interesting thing that happened was meeting the man who would become my favourite teacher. Anthony Luyken came to STM that year and taught science until 1988 when he moved away. He was so different from all the teachers I had had before him. Not only was he the first black man I had ever seen, but he was young and good looking. All my other teachers had been old and had been at their jobs when my father went to school there. Mr. Luyken was new and interesting. A person could tell he really liked his job. He always smiled and took the extra time to help out students who required it.

Mr. Luyken was big into fitness and from 1985–1988 he coached senior boys' basketball and volleyball, junior boys' volleyball, and track and field. He encouraged me to join the track team in Grade 9 and, with his help, I won a gold medal in high jump. As a coach he was relentless in pushing us to be better and to give it everything we had. Training with him was always interesting, tiring and I always came home feeling like I accomplished something.

Sports are not why I remember him so fondly though. He did something for me that he probably didn't realize he had done. He gave me a voice where before I didn't have one.

I was a very shy kid. As a teenager, it had only gotten worse. My biggest fear was answering questions out loud in class. I would answer the questions posed to me as quickly and quietly as possible and hope life would continue on course. I don't know if it was a conscious decision, but Mr. Luyken took it upon himself to help me overcome this. He would ask a question and when I whispered my reply he would repeat it until I would speak up so that everyone could hear. At the time I thought he was picking on me. In fact, reading old journals finds me complaining about him a lot. Eventually I realized that he was trying to show me that speaking in front of a group of people I had known for years was not something that should cause me stress.

He helped break the cycle. I was shy, therefore didn't speak up in class. The students picked on me because I was shy and an easy target, causing me to become more introverted and so on. First he worked on the shyness, and then he worked on the torment. Without making an issue of it, he easily stopped the other students from picking on me.

I remember one time in particular, I was answering a question and a boy in the front called out, "What's that . . . we can't hear you." Mr. Luyken said to him, "You must really like her to pick on her so much." The boy blushed and turned away from me. I don't think he even looked at me for the rest of the year.

As a teenager, I may have had some not very nice things to say about Mr. Luyken when I was venting, but when I think back about my school years, it's his face and his name that comes to mind first.

If I had to describe him in five words or less, I think those words would be: *approachable, tough, dictation*, (he was the first teacher to dictate notes and it was quite a new experience for all of us), *passionate* (in teaching, coaching and mentoring) and *fun*.

In my 1987 yearbook he wrote: *"Judy, you are one of my favourite persons. I certainly hope that life will always be good to you. Keep smiling."*

Turns out he's one of my favourite persons too and, when I think of him, I am smiling.

He Believed in Me

by Kamal Johal

Glynn Searl
James Fowler High School, Calgary

Growing up in a dysfunctional environment was an ongoing struggle when I was a child. At times it was difficult to try and "fit in" and get good grades. During my childhood years, the support of teachers and guidance counsellors inspired me to become a stronger person and a successful student. The story I am about to share is one of my most memorable experiences about a teacher who made a difference. This story is about someone very special—a teacher who changed my life forever. This teacher story takes place in the 1986–1987 school year at James Fowler High School in Calgary.

In Grade 11, I struggled with Math 20 and quickly got turned off. Soon after that I just accepted the "fact" that I could not do math but I still needed enough credits to graduate from high school. As a result, I had to go into Math 33 in Grade 12 which was the lower stream for those students who did not do well in Math 20.

While in the first semester, my attitude about math began to change. Mr. Searl was kind of cool. I liked the way he laughed and he had a good sense of humour. I also found him very approachable; every time I had a problem or did not pass a test he would tell me "not to worry." A bunch of us would sit in his room at lunch almost every day. It was a nice, quiet place to "hang out." His classroom door was always open; it was a safe place to be during the noon hour. I could talk to Mr. Searl about anything—not just mathematics—and he would tell me that everything would be okay. I did well in Math 33 and got over 80 percent in his class! I wanted to try Math 30 and 31, so I went and asked him for permission to take these courses from him during the second semester. He agreed and allowed me to take both classes. So I had two math classes every day.

At the end of that semester, I successfully completed both math classes. Mr. Searl even helped me apply for university! I hesitated as I filled out the forms;

I never thought I would be accepted. I got early admission—I never would have believed it. My Grade 12 math teacher was a true mentor and thanks to him, my life changed forever. Mr. Searl's students came first, and *then* the subject he was supposed to teach.

Four years ago, Mr. Searl and his wife attended my master's graduation ceremony. He told me that the guidance counsellors from my high school were not happy with him back then for allowing me to take Math 30 and 31. When I asked why, he said that they thought I would not be able to handle the course requirements. But he told me that he believed in me and in my work ethic. Thanks to him I was able to successfully complete the necessary courses for university entrance! At that moment I was so emotional. A split-second decision to allow me to take Math 30 helped me get into university. I still get chills thinking about it. It is just one of those "Wow!" moments that one never forgets.

A teacher can have a tremendous impact on a student's life. I am trying to hold back tears as I reflect back and write this story. He will always be special to me. Thanks, Mr. Searl, for believing in me and for all you did for me during that Grade 12 year.

I am proud to say that I am now working on my PhD in the Faculty of Education at the University of Calgary. I also teach Grade 7 math at a junior high school within the public school system. (I always keep my classroom door "open" for my students during the noon hour!)

He Pointed Me Down Life's Path

by Krista Deregowski

Denis Routhier
École Frère Antoine French Immersion School, Edmonton

1988 was Mr. Denis Routhier's first year of teaching at École Frère Antoine French Immersion School in Edmonton, and he was my Grade 2 teacher.

Mr. Routhier had a unique way of teaching that I have not experienced since. His style had us believe we were teaching him, rather than the other way around. I remember learning about fractions and his telling us that one half was "un dummy," and we shouted out several times, "Non, Monsieur, c'est un *demi*," trying to convince our teacher that he was saying it wrong.

In preparation for our weekly spelling

Denis Routhier. *Courtesy: Krista Deregowski*

bees, Mr. Routhier would give us a list of new words and call upon some students to read them aloud. He asked one of the smartest kids in our class, David, to read the word, "N-O-N," which David correctly read as, "Non." This led to a back-and-forth exchange between Mr. Routhier and David, with Mr. Routhier saying, "David, please read the word," and David answering, "Non," and the rest of us laughing and wondering why Mr. Routhier just didn't understand.

But Mr. Routhier was more than just humour in the classroom; he was there to point his students in the right direction in life. At least, that's what he did for me.

When I was in elementary school, I loved math and simply couldn't get enough of it. I was always one of the top students in class, so my marks were never a concern. However, one particular reporting period, all of my marks were characteristically high except for my mark in writing.

At the parent/teacher interview, my parents requested I be given an opportunity to work ahead in math. However, Mr. Routhier suggested it might be better to focus my efforts on increasing my writing skills. He told my parents that I excelled at everything, but that he felt my writing skills were not at the same level as my other skills. He suggested that when I finished my work, I should practice writing stories.

That was it for me. Although I still liked math, it got put aside in favour of a pink notebook and a pencil. It was that year that I decided what I was going to do with the rest of my life—I was going to be a writer.

Through the remaining ten years of my grade school career, I focused on languages. I read and wrote stories just for fun. I wrote my first short story in Grade 7, which my teacher read to my excited class. Writing was my "thing" and everyone knew it. In Grade 8, I had to read a story aloud and one of the tough boys in the class said, "Yea, a Krista story. I know this is going to be good."

I was enrolled in the Advanced English program in high school and in Grade 12, I got my first big break—I was given my own periodical column in the *Edmonton Journal*, writing reviews of entertainment aimed at teens. I have since earned my diploma in journalism, written for a weekly newspaper and am currently working as a communications specialist for a school division.

The thing I am most proud of is that Mr. Routhier knows what I'm doing today and he knows that it's because of him.

Mr. Routhier continues to teach at École Frère Antoine, though he has since moved up to Grade 4. My parents' neighbours have a son who was in his class last year and in talking with them, I heard nothing but praise for Mr. Routhier. Through the years, he has continued to reach his students through humour, as he did with my class those sixteen years ago. But for me the reward was much more than a goofy, memorable school year.

In Grade 2, at the age of eight, Mr. Routhier gently pointed me down my life's path. For that, I am forever grateful.

The Amazing Aussie
by Jennifer Leanne Burnand

Max Foran
Prince of Wales Elementary School, Calgary

The year was 1989 and it was my first day of Grade 6. I was feeling very confident, as I was finally at the top of the school. No older brother to bug me; no bullies I couldn't handle; it was the perfect year. I expected it to be full of fun and excitement. As I sat and pondered how the year might turn out, in walked my new teacher. He was the tallest, proudest man I had ever seen. Suddenly my self-assurance faded as I sank into my seat. Who was this and what was I in for? This couldn't possibly be my teacher for the year. Teachers are supposed to be sweet

Max Foran and Jennifer Burnand.
Courtesy: Jennifer Burnand

little ladies who say only nice things to you—aren't they? I thought there must have been a mistake, but there was no error. He was it; my new teacher for a whole year. Little did I know that Grade 6 would actually end up being the most incredible and memorable year of my academic life.

My teacher, Dr. Maxwell Foran, was the principal of the school and born and raised in Australia. I knew he was tough; I had heard. As I had anticipated, I found the first few days of my Grade 6 year very difficult. Dr. Foran expected so much from us. It even seemed that he expected an exceptional amount from me in particular. It wasn't fair. Why did I get stuck in that class? He always called on us when we weren't paying attention. He even told us he would pick someone to answer if nobody volunteered. Could a kid not just be a kid anymore? Why did school have to be so hard?

One day I realized that my homework was always getting done. I had answers to give, and comments to make in class. I found my hand shooting up in the air as fast as it could, in hopes that I might be called upon for an answer. By the end of the year I had been in competition with myself to fill up my achievement awards. My confidence began to soar. In past years I had phone calls home reminding my mom that I was a social butterfly. I was constantly getting into trouble and really had no reason to change. That year I had calls home letting my mom know how wonderful I was doing. What a change. The year I spent in Dr. Foran's class was the year that I started my future in which I emerged as both a learner and a teacher.

Over ten years later I was flipping through my old school memorabilia and I came across a book that once meant so much to me. It was the language arts notebook that I had saved from Grade 6. It had been my guide to everything I ever needed to know about the English language, and then some. I was now in university and, believe it or not, I used that book to help jog my memory of something I had forgotten. How could a book I wrote in at age eleven, help me in university? It did and I still have it today. That tiny little notebook is a continual reminder that I spent my Grade 6 year trying to achieve the potential that Dr. Foran saw in me.

It wasn't until later in life that I fully realized how much of an impact Dr. Foran had on my life. He consistently went above and beyond for his students, teaching with such enthusiasm and interest that I could never forget him

As I enter a career in teaching, I can only hope to reach even one student in the way that Dr. Maxwell Foran was able to reach me. I owe much of my academic and life successes to the man that forced me to find my own potential and helped me become the person I am today.

Teaching is Lifelong Learning

by Sandra Hart

Kally Krylly
Dr. E.P. Scarlett High School, Calgary

"A lot", "nice", "quite", "good"; these are just a sample of the words on Ms. Krylly's prohibited word list. Ms. Kally Krylly was my English teacher from 1989 to 1992 at Dr. E.P. Scarlett High School in Calgary.

I was uncertain about what to expect when a young woman, with a crew cut and blond bangs, boundless energy and a perpetual pencil behind her ear, sprang into the room. I soon discovered that I was blessed to be in the classroom of a remarkable teacher. Ms. Krylly is an amazing woman who has had a profound influence on my life. Her prohibited words were not the product of a teacher's pet peeves or picky prose choices. They were representative of her mission to inspire excellence in her students' writing. Nearly sixteen years after seeing "the list" for the first time, I still cannot use those words without a cringe of guilt!

In Ms. Krylly's class I learned that Shakespeare's plays are passionate and *funny*. I was educated about Bloom's taxonomy and challenged to use higher levels of critical thinking. I learned what feminism was and its power as a positive agent for change. I learned the name of the Hindu goddess of destruction. I discovered that an optimistic outlook trumps a negative one on every occasion. I adopted the term "lifelong learner" because it was a label Ms. Krylly gave herself. She once told me she became a teacher because she never wanted to stop learning. I completed a Bachelor of Education degree for the same reason.

I have heard many stories recounting the one teacher who made the difference by taking a personal interest in his or her students. Kally Krylly was my special teacher. She cared about me and her other students, beyond the confines of three 65-minute English classes per week. One spring, Ms. Krylly invited my entire English class to spend the weekend at her cabin in Montana. As we sat in companionable silence on the drive there, she suddenly asked, "What are you thinking?" A simple question and yet the memory has stayed with me because it was such a surprise that an adult was interested in what I thought. At a time when I was swimming in a teenage sea of self-doubt, Ms. Krylly was my lighthouse. She shone warm beams of acceptance and support into my life. I still have the many encouragement cards she gave me throughout our time together.

Ms. Krylly also believed in all of her students, enough to challenge us not to accept mediocrity. Although I have gone on to three post-secondary degrees, I have never been as stretched in my capabilities as during those years in high school English. Ms. Krylly poured out as much effort as she expected from her students, co-editing draft after draft until both student and teacher were satisfied with the final product. Language and communication skills, oral and written, are crucial to success and taking pleasure from books makes life sweeter. Kally Krylly laid a rock solid foundation in both these areas to build upon in all of my future endeavours, including my current vocation as a writer.

Thank you, Ms. Krylly.

Chapter 8
Teachers of Today and Tomorrow, 1990–2005

These last fifteen years saw Alberta teachers continue the valuable work of their predecessors over the past century of provincehood. This chapter includes story after story of teachers who played crucial roles in the academic, vocational and life preparation of their students. In classrooms from second grade to high-school graduation, from language arts and social studies through cosmetology and Math 31, we meet "miracle workers" who prodded, encouraged, inspired, and brought out the best in their young charges.

Again, this chapter also reveals the number of Alberta students who were so inspired by their teachers that they, in turn, became teachers and teacher-aides. Thus the torch, the symbolic lamp of learning, is handed down from one generation to the next; passed from the 20th to the 21st century. Read about the work of Terry Susut, Blaise Young, Bernadette McGowan, Cheryl Strauss, Mark Heinricks, Stephen Moses, Ken May, Don Galloway, Theresa Hamilton, Arthur Milan, Marilyn Wickenheiser, and Bev Fleming.

The year 2005 marks the centennial of teacher education in the province of Alberta, with the Faculty of Education at the University of Calgary tracing its roots back to the 1905-06 origins of the Calgary Normal School. How to keep attracting top candidates into teaching and how best to prepare them for the realities of the classroom? These questions are as important for the province in 2005 as they were one hundred years ago. Alberta needs twenty-first century teachers blessed with the talents of the twentieth-century teachers portrayed in this anthology.

A Miracle Worker

by Dave Madole

Terry Susut
Lacombe Composite High School, Lacombe

When I think of Terry Susut, I remember a sun-soaked classroom in the southwest corner of Lacombe Composite High School. I remember the second semester of the 1993 graduating year—my graduating year. I remember a stern, balding man in his mid-forties. I remember a veteran English teacher who looked like he wouldn't give an inch. To me it seemed it would be a dismal semester from the start.

For the first few weeks of class I chose to fly under the radar. It wasn't long however, before Mr. Susut's irrepressible enthusiasm for the English language got a hold of me. Soon I was staying after class to ask about assignments and to talk about anything at all.

In his classes there were portfolios of poetry, scratchy LPs of Robert Frost, and a plethora of presentations in front of the class. In one such presentation I remember floating to the front of the room in a nervous haze, notes rattling in my hand. When I began to speak my voice cracked into an embarrassing pitch. I expected the worst from my peers. There wasn't even a guffaw. I glanced back at Mr. Susut and he gave a reassuring nod so I continued on. No one dared even to squeak. At times like these it was especially wonderful to have a tough yet understanding teacher.

I should mention that Mr. Susut was more than just a teacher to me. Only three years prior my life had taken a turn for the worse. My father had passed away suddenly and the catastrophe sent my life spinning beyond control. In my Grade 11 year, all my marks were mostly failing. I scarcely wanted to be alive, let alone learn anything. I am not hyperbolizing when I say it wasn't a teacher that brought my slide to a halt; it was a miracle worker.

In his class there were expectations to be met no matter how shattered one felt, but there was also encouragement. He never let anyone struggle alone. He talked me through book reports, essays and poetry. He reasoned that, yes, he supposed a title could have a higher word count than the poem beneath it. And, in one of my favourite memories of him, he made exceptions to his usual sternness when circumstances warranted it.

My last remaining vice was leaving school at lunch to watch episodes of *Tiny Toons* with a friend. The only problem was the mad dash to get back to class on time. One day we were so late arriving, we hit the ground running. As we raced, my friend pulled on my backpack to slow me down. While falling I reached up and grabbed her ankle to bring her to a standstill. We became so self-involved that we burst noisily into Mr. Susut's otherwise quiet class. There was the briefest of pauses in his lecture. We held our breath and stared at him blankly. His eyes seemed to smile back at us. Then he resumed his lesson and we took our seats. Sitting breathless in my desk, and to this day, I've appreciated that he didn't merely tolerate the idiosyncrasies of youth. He loved them.

I went on to graduate without complications. At the year-end awards ceremony I was surprised to receive the most improved student award from none other than Terry Susut. We've remained in touch throughout the twelve years since I've graduated. I've even stopped by the school unannounced from time to time. Not as noisily as in the past, mind you.

I graduated from the University of Alberta in the winter of 1998. I've been an English teacher for six years now, and I'm proud to say Terry inspired me in my career choice as well. As he nears retirement, we still share ideas about curriculum and kids. I've asked to be invited to his retirement party, but he insists there won't be one. He's not one to draw attention to himself. Terry is, beyond a doubt, the light for my journey as an educator. Lord knows, with twenty-four years until my retirement, I'll need it, but who's counting?

I Remember So Much of What He Taught

by Jody Sayna

Blaise Young
Forestburg School, Forestburg

When I thought about my most memorable teacher during the years I attended Forestburg School in small-town Alberta, I had a great deal of difficulty narrowing it down to the one who inspired me most. I was fortunate, in such a small rural community, to have many exceptional and gifted teachers, but my most memorable teacher was Blaise Young.

I was fortunate to have him as a teacher from Grade 7 through to Grade 12. He taught me social studies for six years and a vibrant six years it was. I don't remember feeling any special affinity for the subject . . . that is until I entered his class.

Some people tell me they don't remember much about their school days and what they do remember are often things that occurred outside of the classroom, but not me. How could you forget a teacher who strolled down the hallways singing *Strangers in the Night* nearly every day sounding little, if anything, like Frank Sinatra? How could you not look back and laugh at all those times when he would awaken sleeping students by smacking their desks with a metre stick and then blaming it on "those darn fruit flies." It is really a wonder that he didn't go through dozens of metre sticks each year. He had a running policy that the only students allowed to sleep in class were those who received 100 percent on the last quiz. He honoured this policy too; though it seems to me that he only had to honour it twice in six years. He had a habit of creating the most interesting multiple-choice questions by including "revised" versions of the math teacher's name as possible answers—I hate to admit it, but he may have caught me on that once in Grade 7. His lessons were nothing short of captivating. In fact I recall in

Grade 11 that he re-enacted the entire French Revolution for us—all by himself. He was definitely a one-man show, and the best I've seen at that.

But all that aside, I remember so much of what he taught me. In Grade 8, I will never forget having to give a presentation to the class on a famous Canadian. I chose Emily Carr. I was petrified and while I enjoyed the research part of it, I despised the idea of standing before my peers. Looking back, it was a lacklustre presentation; I had sweaty palms, red cheeks and my knees were shaking. However, I will always respect him for forcing us to do it because it taught me to continue to explore my boundaries; to strive, to excel. I remember everything he taught about responsible government in Canada, his colourful descriptions of Rasputin and how he made the issue of Quebec separation come alive for me. I even remember many of the comments he made on my essays, his continual efforts to shape me into a better writer, as well as the subsequent pride I felt when I achieved near-perfect marks on position papers. I remember also the grace with which he accepted occasional late assignments and the compassion he showed when we were going through rough times. That, more than anything, is something I endeavour to keep with me.

I am a teacher now; a high-school social studies and English teacher. In a lot of ways, I have him to thank for that. He inspired and shaped my interest in history and social issues, gave me advice on what undergraduate course to enrol in and when I was immersed in much soul-searching after an arduous first year at university (perhaps unbeknownst to him) he turned my life path in a very decisive direction. I had mediocre marks in that first year and was reconsidering my decision to complete a business degree. I approached my uneasy parents with the suggestion that an education degree might be more suitable. After meeting him on the street and mentioning my change of heart, the deal was sealed in my parents' minds when he said, "You have nothing to worry about! She'll make an excellent teacher." Needless to say, I haven't looked back. I can only hope to leave behind the kind of legacy that he will leave once he retires.

Her Unconditional Love Spread Like Wild Roses

by Robbyn Fielding

Bernadette McGowan
Bishop Grandin High School, Calgary

Although I graduated from Bishop Grandin High School in 1997, I still carry my lessons and experiences with me every day. Bernadette McGowan not only taught me to be a great hairdresser, she also educated me about life.

She gave all her students the encouragement and the unconditional love we needed. We needed it because hundreds of people passed through her salon-lab every year—not only students, but clients, teachers, parents, and administrators—and that was a lot for us to handle.

Bernadette McGowan wanted us to understand that although we were still learning, we were running a professional and functioning hair salon. We were expected to work by selling products, handling clients and, of course, by performing our skills. Because of this, many of her graduates have gone on to become successful licensed hairstylists and aestheticians.

With that said, a lot of us would not have had a future without the cosmetology program. As teenagers with many uncontrollable emotions and hormones, we often found ourselves having to account for our various adventures in the confined walls of her office. However, the lectures that occurred within were always delivered with love and compassion. She knew that through honest conversation and guidance we'd usually end up making the right decisions.

This unconditional love spread like wild roses throughout all the classes, and her students came to understand that all communities, not just classrooms, become healthier when built on this kind of support. To drive this point home, Ms. McGowan often involved us in charitable events by requiring us to collect food, clothes, household items, and personal supplies. One year in particular, we got to hand-deliver food hampers to local families-in-need. We all loved it since, in giving to the community, it gave us a sense of togetherness as a classroom as well as a sense of ownership over something good. In keeping with her kind and giving soul, she hoped for us to experience the importance of giving to the underprivileged; and we did.

It wasn't all about community, however. In her classroom it was very important for each person to express his or her individuality. In fact, the idea of "self" was the most important lesson that I took away. It was not always easy, though. In high school, the social pressure to be like everybody else was very pronounced. However, with Ms. McGowan, all judgements were left outside her classroom door, and nobody was allowed to belittle anyone else. This is where I experienced the most growth and began to take root in myself. She taught me that people all experience things differently and, because of this, they may have different reactions. This was a very respectful idea, and we all came to appreciate it. She made a special effort to know each of our unique talents and gave us credit for them. This helped us relate to one another. It also helped us get a grasp on ourselves and allowed us to really look inside. We understood from her example that to be ourselves required constant searching and she gave us the flashlight to do so. Finding our way through the dark tunnels and shadows seemed easier when there was someone else with us. This helped us be honest with ourselves and others, and many close friendships developed in the classroom because of this. At the time I didn't realise how deep the self was, but in carrying these lessons and experiences with me every day since my time at Bishop Grandin, I have begun to. Thanks, Ms. McGowan!

We Called Her Strauss

by Brittany Wickerson

Cheryl Strauss
Woodman Junior High School, Calgary

"That is what learning is. You suddenly understand something you've under-stood all your life, but in a new way." (Doris Lessing, *The Four-Gated City*)

I am reminded of when I was in Grade 8 at Woodman Junior High School in 1998, and I stayed up until eleven-thirty to write my first opinion paper, to show Mrs. Cheryl Strauss how good a writer I really was.

"Strauss", as we affectionately called her, inspired me and propelled me upwards towards things I had not imagined. She encouraged me to write, and not just in class, or for school, but for me. I have filled journals and journals in the years since then. Writing has got me through some difficult times and the words continue to support me; even as I write this I remember going home and writing until I was exhausted, but I digress. In Grade 7, I was sent to the guid-ance counsellor for a story I had written on the given topic of "A Bad Day" (well what do people expect?). The next year, in Strauss' class, she taught me one of the most important lessons I'll ever learn: they just weren't ready for you. Suddenly it was okay for me to write poetry and position papers on abortion, when most of my classmates had never heard of Somerset Maugham.

Strauss made you want to work, not even to get the marks, or because you had to, but because there was some sort of satisfaction you got from working hard and getting the recognition you always thought you deserved. She culti-vated my passion, and I do tend to be a very passionate, dramatic girl, in a way that no other teacher has. I remember only once that I ever slacked off in her class and when she came to me in the hall during lunch, and asked why (it was to impress a boy, by the way), I felt so guilty, I never did it again.

Cheryl Strauss made it worthwhile to do your best, she was always tossing around candy and over-praising the really good pieces of work handed in. I don't know of anyone in her classes who ever disliked her or her lessons; we always did a lot of laughing for that hour.

She had a wall, filled with pictures of her students and her two sons, and there was nothing better than making it up on that wall, and though I like to think she played favourites with me, I think it more the reverse, because she loved all her students, or at least the ones while I was there. Everyone got noticed; everyone got special treatment from her.

For Christmas, our school had an assembly where some of the students could go up on stage and receive "gifts" from Santa, and that year Strauss gave a less well-behaved student a cat collar with a bell so that "all the girls will hear you coming". It sent the audience into laughter and for all the looks the guy who got the gift made, he was actually quite pleased. I think every student will remember Strauss running through the hallways with her camera, dressed in psychedelic, hippie garb and using that loud voice of hers to get our attention.

When we read *The Outsiders* in class she said to me that the book was written by a 16-year-old, and that hopefully I'd have a book out by then. I don't, but if I ever get one out there, her name will be in the dedication. She didn't just teach me, she made me see in myself what I and others couldn't, or didn't want to, see.

The Heinricks' Effect
by Dana Schattle

Mark Heinricks
Eagle Butte High School, Dunmore

Sometimes things just work out. Somehow the stars align, the heavens open, the birds sing, and things happen the way they were meant to happen. It probably was not that profound the day that Mark Heinricks decided to be a teacher, but to his future students, it would mean a night and day difference for how they would learn *math*. Some people have described him as having "a gift" and that he is not only an invaluable resource to his school and his district, but also to his students.

The first year that our paths crossed was 1994 at Alexandra Junior High School in Medicine Hat. By then he was married, had two of his four children, and was one of the best math teachers in the province. I was in Grade 7, and I never was lucky enough to have him as a teacher, but he was already gaining his reputation back then.

During my Grade 9 year, I heard that he had left Alexandra, and was teaching at this brand new school named Eagle Butte High School. Naturally, when I enrolled in EBHS, I hoped I'd be lucky enough to experience his teaching. When I got there, I found that he had again moved jobs to go to Irvine School where I had just graduated from. Fate was just not working in my favour! So, during my Grade 11 year, the first day of school, whom should I see, but none other than Mr. Heinricks back at EBHS to take over his old job! I quickly decided to take Math 20 and Math 30 in the same year, so that I would be sure to be in his Math 30 class, and it worked!

He was one of the most inspiring teachers I'd ever had the pleasure to know. I was one of his top students, and yet he still pulled me in for extra help if I got less than 90 percent on an exam. He was not one of those teachers who looked for that magical 65 percent class average, and was happy with that. Mark knew what each of us was capable of, and if we didn't live up to his expectations, he let us know. To me, that is a sign of a great teacher.

It is because of his class that I am in my final semester of the Teacher Education Program at the University of Lethbridge, completing my final practicum at the same school where I was Mark's student. Now I'm his colleague, and that is something I've always wanted to be.

It's been a long road to where I am today; striving for excellence, which is a symptom of "The Heinricks' Effect". Every teacher within an eighty kilometre radius of Eagle Butte High School has heard of him, and is dying to know his secrets: How do you make Math 30 Pure fun? How do you keep them interested? How do you do it? The answer is that he was *meant* to be a teacher. To this day, when he pats me on the back and says "Good job, Dana," I know I've done it. I knew that as Mark's math student, and now as a math teacher in my own right, I know it even better. "The Heinricks' Effect" has influenced so many others as well as me over many years; it has become an institution at Eagle Butte High School. Despite all of his success, Mark remains a humble person, who loves to joke around with his students, and is an accomplished coach of the varsity basketball team.

He is an amazing teacher, a great colleague, and a remarkable father. My only hope for the future is that I can be half the person that he is now.

He Cared Enough to Make Phone Calls

by Chian Shyan Leong

Stephen Moses
John G. Diefenbaker High School, Calgary

In my twelve years of education I have been fortunate enough to cross paths with teachers who have impacted my life by pushing me beyond my potential with their consistent encouragement and boundless well of support when I had lost all faith in my abilities. The teacher I was blessed with who helped me in Applied Math 20 was Mr. Moses. Being the caring teacher he was he would always go an extra mile to help his students achieve their goals.

Over and over, I've been told that in order for one to be successful, their presence in class is crucial. Along with attending every lecture, a great attitude is needed—knowing one will live up to one's full potential by doing the best an individual can do will contribute to propelling that person towards their goal. A bonus in obtaining one's goal is by having outstanding teachers who really use all they can to help their students to acquire their goals.

Most times, I think teachers' efforts go unnoticed and students take them for granted. Mr. Moses really stressed the importance of being in class, because he knew how vital it was to our success. Therefore, whether a student was really sick and couldn't be in class, or chose to skip, he would always make a point of calling the individual's home to find out why the student decided not to attend class. He liked inquiring about the student's whereabouts, so the next time the student would want to skip, they would think twice about whether they wanted to receive another phone call home. Most students really despised this caring act because most teachers wouldn't bother to concern themselves. However, seeing him take his time out of his schedule to call people who were absent showed me how lucky I was to stumble across a teacher who cared enough to spend his time making phone calls.

Mr. Moses liked incorporating jokes and was always ready to share one of his life stories with his students. He had the ability to create a really enjoyable atmosphere to be in which motivated me to want to attend class everyday. As the semester was coming to an end, Mr. Moses had his students write about the things they liked and disliked about him as a teacher, and the papers remained anonymous. I've never met a teacher who cared so much about the students that he wanted criticism from them and used these insights to improve himself. By doing this, he would become a better teacher to future students.

One day I was having a bad day and Mr. Moses took notice. He approached me after teaching his lesson and asked if I was okay. He went on to insist that, if I wanted, I could take a walk out in the hallway. Never in my life had a teacher taken notice about the way I felt and taken the time to really acknowledge it and do whatever he could in his power to help make my day better.

When a person looks back and thinks about why some teachers had such an imprint upon their life, I believe it's because of the way they made them feel as a student. To this day, I am still so grateful for the opportunity to be one of Mr. Moses' students. The privilege of knowing what it was like to have a teacher, who always went out of their way to make you, as an individual feel cared for as a student, is a gift in itself.

Dad Made Math 31 My Favourite Class

by Shannon MacMillan

Ken May
Winston Churchill High School, Lethbridge

Ken and Mary May. *Courtesy: Shannon MacMillan*

My most memorable Alberta teacher taught me Math 31 (calculus) in my final semester of high school. It was the winter semester of 1990 at Winston Churchill High School in Lethbridge. My teacher's name was Ken May or, outside of class, better known to me as *Dad*. I was nervous, concerned and excited to be entering my dad's class for the first time—nervous because I was not entirely sure how the other students would treat me as the daughter of the teacher; concerned that Ken May might be harder on his own daughter than the other students; and excited after twelve years of education to finally have my father as a teacher.

My worries were unwarranted and Math 31 ended up being my favourite class and one I looked forward to each day. I learned not only the basics of calculus, but also how learning could be fun. Dad made calculus interactive by getting us up to the chalkboard solving math problems and really learning from one another. Although this was intimidating at first, it became part of the fun and experience of class. My father's energy and enthusiasm became contagious. He motivated us to learn and to always aspire higher. Dad allowed us to experience things that were not only focused on calculus. He was the only teacher in my Grade 12 year who agreed to have post-secondary representatives come and talk to our class because our futures were important to him and he wanted us to be aware of the options available to us.

Although calculus was the subject we were focused on that semester, I also learned some helpful life lessons—like skipping math class when your dad is the teacher is not a wise thing to do! The only class I skipped throughout my high school years was one class of Math 31. I thought I might get off easy as the daughter of the teacher—but I was wrong. This was when I really came to understand another life lesson about treating everyone as equals. My father treated me like everyone else in the class and I learned something about the value of treating people as equals with fairness and respect.

I also learned that humour is something that reaches everyone and laughing is contagious; hard work combined with a good laugh makes the work seem less tedious. I do not believe there was a calculus class I attended where my father did not have a smile on his face and a joke or laugh to share with us. I observed him answer endless questions with patience and kindness and learned that how you relate to people, and respect their individual needs will earn you the highest levels of respect in return. I learned that honesty, dedication and loyalty are values to live by not only in your personal life, but in your career as well. I saw this demonstrated as he spent hours with his students (including myself), outside of the classroom helping to solve the most difficult calculus problems. He challenged us and made us want to succeed and in turn make him proud. All these lessons were learned through my father's approach to each class he taught. The values that he holds in high regard were brought with him into the classroom and as his students, we benefited from this.

I am more fortunate than my peers who shared only one semester learning from my father, as I continue to learn from him on a daily basis. I am proud to know that countless students were turned onto math, or education, or life, thanks to my dad. Excellent teachers make incredible differences in the lives of their students. Thank you Dad for sharing your passions for math, learning and life with me.

His Sense of Humour was Intoxicating

by Jamie-Dee Peterson

Don Galloway
Samuel Crowther Middle School, Strathmore

Throughout my life as a student I have had approximately 110 teachers. This spans Kindergarten to Grade 12 and through my university career. It is truly incredible how many teachers it takes to get one student through school. I have been blessed with incredible teachers and have many stories to tell. However, there is one individual who has stood out for me since the moment I met him.

He was standing in the foyer at Samuel Crowther Junior High School hollering at students as they walked by. I remember thinking, "That must be him. I have heard about him." And before I could hide my face and get past him without noticing, he said, "Well, well, Ms. Peterson has entered the building." I was absolutely mortified. He went on to say, extremely loudly so every student in the foyer could hear, "You have a lot to live up to my darling!" I tried to walk as fast as I could and stay far, far away from Mr. Galloway.

I learned very quickly that staying away from Mr. Galloway was virtually impossible. Not only did he seem to be everywhere, but he had charisma that drew students to him. He had an uncanny ability to connect with every student; he gave them a voice and place where they were safe and excited to be. His sense of humour was intoxicating and he always left you with something to think about. Although Mr. Galloway never taught me in the classroom, he taught me on the volleyball court, in the hallways, after school, throughout my high school years and into adulthood. He is such an amazing man and he has made a great impact on my life.

To narrow down one story about Mr. Galloway is virtually impossible, so I will share just a few. When I moved on to high school, Mr. Galloway and I kept in touch through letters, telephone calls, and conversations over coffee. Each month we would get together and I would update him on the latest gossip and the major crisis of the moment. He always listened, never judged and offered fatherly advice.

In 1995, when I was in Grade 11, he had a heart attack. Without any thought, three friends and I made our way to the Foothills Hospital ICU. After a short visit, my friends allowed me some time with Mr. Galloway. I wasn't really sure what to say to him but I knew that someone had to give him the straight-up truth. So, I gave it to him. Don and his wife do not have any children, but I felt that he was such a huge part of my life, and I in his that he needed to know what was going through my head. I told him I was not going to have him die on me before he could see me graduate high school, get through university, be married and, most of all, see his adopted grandchildren. And through all of this, as always, his was a pillar of strength.

He went on to make my high school graduation memorable as our guest speaker. He made mention of each and every student and how important their role was. That day, he encouraged all of us to go forth and conquer. He is truly a remarkable man.

More than anything, he has taught the importance of connecting with students and maintaining those relationships. I have been extremely fortunate to continue my friendship with Mr. Galloway to this day. I have cherished each moment and every memory with him. He has made me a better person and encourages me every day to become an even better teacher. I am proud to be a part of the teaching profession and only hope that I can leave such lasting impressions as Mr. Galloway has left with me.

She Opened the Windows

by Steven Peters

Theresa Hamilton
St. Anthony's School, Drumheller

Few people will claim that an event, at 8 years of age, changed his or her life. Yet often, in retrospect, the hills climbed and the falls fallen are smaller than what one remembers, the fashions somehow less important, and the days longer and more exciting. Still, the early days are some of the most important. That said some teachers are in the business of planting seeds, knowing that they won't necessarily be there to watch the seed break through the soil, the first leaves, the first flower. And since we always seem to prefer to remember the twists and turns in the road and not what got us on the road in the first place, it's often only in retrospect that we appreciate the more subtle areas.

Mrs. Hamilton wasn't subtle in most ways. Looking back, she enjoyed bright-coloured fashions and shiny jewellery. She always had a gigantic smile, as though she truly loved every minute of her life. And her voice could always be heard far across the hall, with a power and projection that defied her short stature. Yet the success of her teaching lay in the silent way she directed us, and taught us to be more than little kids.

The memories of the third grade are like still-frames, a shuffled deck of photographs or 20-second movie clips with audio tracks badly damaged. Looking through the deck I hear her heartfelt laughter, see her giant smile in response to a student's request for early recess. I remember the baby ducks that occasionally slipped out of their pen to join us for class, and the ease with which Mrs. Hamilton would deal with the situation, letting chaos run its course just long enough for every child to have a view and a laugh before she effortlessly reinstated order. I remember the paints gone astray on the floor and her cheerful response to the cleanup, the fun of working at learning centres on Tuesdays (or was it Wednesdays?). Such specific memories aren't what

222

made her special; what she left her students wasn't anything nearly so palpable. Her essence can't be summed up in cute anecdotes or speeches inspiring a class of graduates.

Something I only appreciate now is that she developed a system, a method to teach the curriculum and still leave time for development, to see how each child grew, encouraging and accepting the idiosyncrasies of each child: the rambunctious athlete forever talking at inopportune times, the burgeoning writer always daydreaming when asked a question, the fanciful artist drawing castles on math worksheets, the engineer making catapults of pencils and elastic bands. What she added was independence, self reliance, and reinforcement of those things that made a child proud. "Why, why! Look at you!" she'd assert, seemingly genuinely admiring a drawing and adjusting her bracelets. "What do you want to do next?" and the child would be off to tackle a new project.

With Mrs. Hamilton there was no lasting rebuke; there was no need. After a spirited snowball fight at recess, I remember being told simply and firmly that it wasn't allowed and that we knew that. There was no need to belittle the point. She said it once and every guilty party hung his head and sincerely felt shame. Enough said, a laugh and a nudge and you had promised to never do it again, and soon you were lining up at the door for gym class, or putting your books neatly in your desk as she had showed you, or following intently the math problems on the board.

She taught, watched, coaxed, gave space. She was not just a teacher. Few critical facts, if not learned in the third grade, will not be learned elsewhere. Helping us become little people was much more important, and in this way she was a facilitator, expander, road builder. Like Miss Stacy, in *Anne of Green Gables*, she "opened the windows" for some young minds and for a couple of generations she made space for a step from kids to individual people.

Perhaps there were others like her. I only know that she was an institution at St. Anthony's, and she moulded the spirits of many who never even realized it. She will be happily remembered as someone who brought out the best in each of us before we even had an idea of what that best was.

A Perfect Role Model

by Pauline (MacCallum) Lamontagne

Arthur Milan
Our Lady of Mount Carmel School, Edmonton

Arthur Milan. *Courtesy: Pat Milan*

Mount Carmel School, Edmonton 1991 . . . and I was miserable. Several years later, I realized the great gift I had been given in my teacher, Mr. Arthur Milan.

It all started out fine—I was no longer a small-town girl—I was going to start fresh in a REAL city school. I knew just how to style my hair and I had the brand new slouch socks and black jeans all laid out on the bed, ready to start my exciting birth into new books, new friends and wonderful memories. Was I ever wrong!

The clothes and hair worked for the first few weeks but soon the realities of my life quickly overtook the fresh start I was trying desperately to make. My home situation was in major disarray; I wasn't as pretty or as popular as I thought I should be, and I was never in the mood to work.

As a new Grade 8 band student, I needed to meet with Mr. Milan to pick my instrument. Being as shy as I was, I wound up selecting the loudest possible instrument to learn: the trumpet. I enjoyed the idea of playing the thing until I realized in my first band class that music (to my dismay) often has solo parts featuring the trumpet throughout the piece. Over the next two years instead of complaining or getting frustrated, Mr. Milan played all the trumpet parts along with me everyday, providing encouragement and support. At the same time, he conducted the entire band with baton and trumpet in hand.

English class was also a challenge. I loved to read but I couldn't stand the idea of being critiqued for something I worked hard on and then wind up with a less than desirable mark. My solution—don't write anything! I'm sure this drove him crazy but again I was only shown kindness and understanding. Mr. Milan would talk to me after school about the books we were reading in class and the questions that had been given for homework. I would answer him orally and that's how I completed English in junior high.

I didn't ever want to leave after school. Things at home for me were very dysfunctional so I would visit with teachers and wander the halls hours after the day was completed. Mr. Milan let me hang out in the band room where I perfected walking on my hands across the floor, plunked away at the piano for fun or occasionally even practiced my trumpet parts. Sometimes he would visit with me and sometimes I would be alone—but that room was my safe place where I could just be me.

I was angry with him once and I kicked him HARD in the shins while wearing steel-toed boots. (He says he can still see the scar). My surprise was his response. He didn't yell at me or run to the principal. He just quietly and gently asked me to go. The next day he acted as though nothing had happened.

Looking back, I realize that the great gift I had been given was unconditional love and acceptance. My actions in many respects did not deserve that, but it was shown to me anyway. I was given the perfect role model for two years that I, as a young girl, desperately needed. He didn't yell, criticize or judge me. He taught me patience, gentleness and understanding. Mr. Milan knew I was worth the effort. I was the one that needed to believe it.

Now as a teacher assistant, I want the students that I work with to know they're worth it. Through him I was shown that silence is often the loudest teacher and knowing someone believes in you even when you can't is a great and precious gift.

Thank you Mr. Milan, for saving my life. I knew when I went to sleep at night that I would be all right and the next day would be okay. I knew that because I would wake up in the morning and return to school where I would find an amazing teacher who loved and believed in me over and over again.

The Dandelion
by Felicia Pacentrilli

Marilyn Wickenheiser
St. Hubert Elementary School, Calgary

Class of '93. Marilyn Wickenheiser (rear left) and Felicia Pacentrilli (front row – 3rd from right).
Courtesy: Felicia Pacentrilli

"Okay class, read the poem carefully, then write down what you think the poet intended the title to be." Silence quickly enveloped the room, as blank stares bounced off the walls, and pencil erasers were maliciously chewed. I slowly read it over, once, twice, allowing it to form in my mind. I loved English, and read many books, so the image quickly came to me. I proudly printed the title in my awkward scrawl, as the rest of the class continued working, throwing the words around in their minds.

It was the school year of 1992–93, during a bright afternoon in April at St. Hubert's Elementary. I was a shy, red-faced little girl in a Grade 2/3 split, taught by Mrs. Wickenheiser. Looking back in time, I can still clearly see her dark, bright eyes framed by her dainty oval spectacles, and our little classroom, flooded with light.

We were arranged in groups of four, desks haphazardly shoved together, a mixture of 7- and 8-year-olds. I watched as Mrs. Wickenheiser surveyed the room, as she often did, glancing up and down the aisles. Finally she stopped in front of me, noted my answer and gave me a wide, knowing smile. Pleased, I looked to my three companions to see what was taking them so long. Letting my eyes wander, I became a little puzzled when I noticed the older girl next to me had a completely different answer. Hoping to reaffirm my response, I scanned the paper of the girl across from me, yet she had the same answer as the girl beside me. In fact, all the older kids in my group had spelled out "soldier", instead of "dandelion", and I felt my cheeks glow furiously. Perhaps my teacher's smile had masked a laugh when she saw how silly my answer was, and since the older kids took longer and had the same answer, I had to be wrong. Hastily, I scrubbed away the remnants of "dandelion", and jotted "soldier", before anyone noticed.

Finally, Mrs. Wickenheiser threaded her way back to the front, and slyly looked around hoping an answer would be offered. I firmly cast my eyes down, which was always a bit dangerous when you didn't want to be called on, especially in Mrs. Wickenheiser's class! Eventually, she chose someone, who proudly called out "soldier", to which

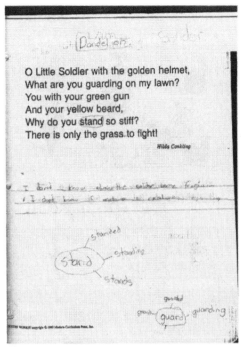

The Dandelion. *Courtesy: Felicia Pacentrilli*

Mrs. W., shook her head no, still smiling with her eyes, and pointed to another, who firmly reasserted that the poem was indeed referring to a soldier. Again, Mrs. W., said no. I had an uneasy feeling that I might be next. Even with eyes downcast, you always knew when the teacher was staring at you. I gulped as I heard her call my name.

"Why don't you share your answer with the class?" Everyone waited expectantly. I knew I could mumble out "soldier" for the third time, or just say "dandelion". Mrs. Wickenheiser's prodding smile danced upon her face, as I searched her eyes for some encouragement. I would like to say that I then proudly announced, "Dandelion, the answer is dandelion," but unfortunately I didn't have that kind of courage then, so I mumbled out "soldier."

Without speaking, she strode towards me. Everyone watched. "Felicia, what was your first answer," she urged, "your real answer?" I hesitated, remembering the vivid image that had flashed in my mind and my initial certainty. "Dandelion," I finally spoke up. "Yes," she said emphatically. "Yes."

She then walked over to our group and stood right beside me, as she told the whole class how I had the right answer the first time but then changed it. It was mortifying at the time, yet looking back—a defining point.

Here was this tough, imaginative teacher who was raising a future hockey superstar at home, and inspiring a little girl who loved to read, write and imagine at school. We even got to meet her daughter, Hayley, who was about 10 or 12, and hear about her life. Inspiration abounded in class that year; it was an age when little minds were searching, honing. Some found it in Hayley, some found it in friendships and class work, but I found it in *The Dandelion*, and Mrs. Wickenheiser's careful persistence.

Thanks for Listening to Me Cry

by Carla (Cheperdak) Lovell

Bev Fleming
Clover Bar Junior High School, Sherwood Park

This is a thank you to Bev Fleming, my junior high principal from Clover Bar Junior High in Sherwood Park. She taught me Social Studies back in 1992, and I owe her a debt of gratitude for the woman I have become.

Dear Ms. F:

Nineteen ninety-two was the year you got sick. It was the year you taught me social studies in Grade 9, and the year I was finally apprehended by the government and put into foster care. What you taught me in class I have long since forgotten; however, the life lessons you taught me will never be.

I know we had a rocky relationship when you first came to Clover Bar, or "Clover Hole" as it was more affectionately known by us kids. However, as time went on, it became apparent to me that you actually knew a thing or two.

One moment for me was when you had assigned us a social studies project, and a group of us didn't hand it in on time. That morning, you hauled us into the library and chewed us out royally for not being bothered to hand in the assignment. You had said something about scheduling your hospital visits for that morning before classes so you could pick them up and mark them over the weekend. You were wearing a gold-coloured Clover Bar Trojans sweater, and your exact words were, "to heck with you." You had tears in your eyes, and were still sick from your radiation. Those words, as well as the look in your eyes, never lost their effect on me.

The turning point for me in our teacher-student relationship was when, in January 1992, I was apprehended by the Department of Social Services and put into foster care in Ardrossan. I can still remember when I found out that you were the one responsible for keeping me at Clover Bar, and my first thought was that it was to torture me. However, hindsight is 20/20, and I truly think now that you saw something in the skinny punk with green hair and 6-inch bangs that I couldn't see: potential. Someone once told me that great things arise from the ashes. I was to become one of them.

The last day of junior high, we had a little chat in your office, which, by that point, had my own personal chair in it. I apologized to you for my awful behaviour, and you noted to me how much I had improved over the past months since I went into care. Maybe it was just me at 14, or maybe I did see it, but I really got the feeling that you gave a damn about me, which was something at that point I was unfamiliar with.

Three years went by when, in January 1995, I got sick. I remember you coming by the hospital and talking to me after you got off from school one night. Like I said earlier, you must have seen something I couldn't have. Your words gave me the courage to fight back for my life.

Even though we have lost touch, I just wanted to say thank you for having your hand in turning me into the woman I am today. For the record, you may want to know how that skinny punk kid with the green hair turned out.

I lived in Quebec, where I went to university over the summer of 1996. When I came home to Alberta, I could barely speak English. Today, I am still fairly fluent in French. I then moved to Calgary, where I earned my Bachelor of Science degree. Then in 2004, I earned my First Year Apprenticeship in Welding.

All in all Ms. Fleming, I turned out pretty ok, thanks to you.

So thanks for teaching me to fight for what I believe in. Thanks for teaching me that life is more than what you're given. Thanks for listening to me cry, putting up with my crap, giving me hell when I deserved it, giving me praise when I deserved it, and influencing me in a way that no teacher ever matched.

Thanks for having been my teacher.

Index